CW00504287

WALKING IN THE
PENDLE WITCH
COUNTRY
and the West Pennine Moors

A COMPANION GUIDE

Text and photographs by Chris Gee

A CIP catalogue record for this book is available
from the British Library.

ISBN 978 0 85710 116 7

PiXZ Books
Halsgrove House, Ryelands Business Park,
Bagley Road, Wellington, Somerset TA21 9PZ
Tel: 01823 653777
Fax: 01823 216796
email: sales@halsgrove.com

An imprint of Halstar Ltd, part of the
Halsgrove group of companies
Information on all Halsgrove titles is
available at: www.halsgrove.com

Printed in India by
Parksons Graphics

*In memory of my dad Tom who instilled
in me a love of travel and adventure and
with whom I have walked much of this
countryside. I'll always remember the
pint we had in the Royal Arms at Ryal
Fold after walking Darwen Moor.*

*Thanks also to my wife Jo for
accompanying me on day trips, for
her patience when waiting for the sun
to come back out again and for
her proofreading of the text.*

Front cover: Jubilee Tower, Darwen Hill.

Winter Hill sunset from Peel Tower.

CONTENTS

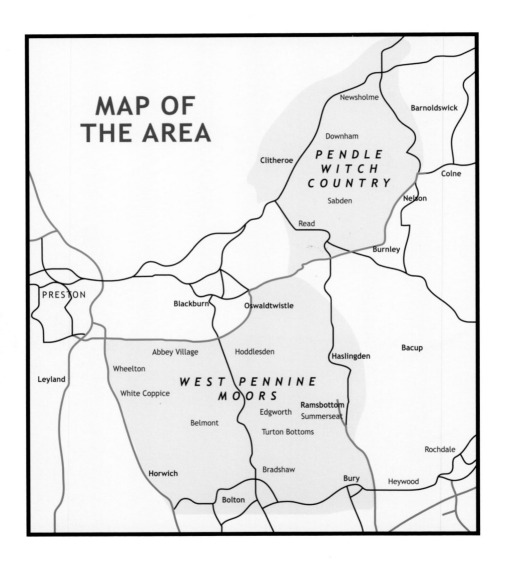

MAP OF THE AREA

Newsholme

Barnoldswick

Downham

PENDLE WITCH COUNTRY

Clitheroe

Colne

Sabden

Nelson

Read

Burnley

PRESTON

Blackburn

Oswaldtwistle

Bacup

Abbey Village

Hoddlesden

Haslingden

Wheelton

Leyland

WEST PENNINE MOORS

White Coppice

Ramsbottom

Edgworth

Summerseat

Belmont

Turton Bottoms

Rochdale

Horwich

Bradshaw

Bury

Heywood

Bolton

Southbound Fellsman crossing Whalley Arches and the River Calder.

INTRODUCTION

I grew up within sight of Lancashire's hill country and ended up going to school in Bolton where the high moors were an ever present backdrop to the terraces and mills of this typical Lancashire town. They became my playground after work in much the same way as they have been for others over the centuries, particularly during and after the industrial revolution. These were the places where millworkers would escape to breathe fresh air in what little leisure time they had away from the workplace.

These moors and hills were much cherished by working class families and ramblers wanting to escape the towns and industry and as such they were in the vanguard of what we now take for granted: access to the countryside. Darwen's Moors were granted to the public long before the concept of the National Trust. Winter Hill became a battleground for the right of access to the countryside long before the more famous Mass Trespass on Kinder Scout in 1932. These moors and hills are still valued today with such a long history of recreational use.

This is a landscape of cotton grass and purple heather, where the haunting call of the curlew, the 'peewit' cry of lapwing and the burbling song of the skylark are your spring and summer soundtrack. On warm summer days this is a great place to be, the sun beating down on baked peat, while the cotton grass bobs in the breeze. In late summer the heather, predominantly ling, will be a purple swathe across the rolling hills. Darwen Moor is perhaps the best place to enjoy the heather in bloom. Small birds like meadow pipits, linnets and reed bunting will flit across the scene. There are rare examples of a floating bog to be discovered.

The natural wealth of this landscape was finally recognised in 2017 when it was declared a Site of Specific Scientific Interest. As the West Pennine Moors are no longer managed for grouse shooting, it has allowed flora and fauna to flourish and has a high level of biodiversity. There are widespread areas of blanket bog on deep peat soils. Notable flora includes purple moor-grass, cotton grass, cross-leaved heath, bog rosemary, cranberry and several species of sphagnum moss.

The reservoirs are home to a wide selection of wintering wildfowl, but it is perhaps the upland areas that are most special, being home to peregrine falcon, merlin, kestrel, short-eared owl, buzzard, golden plover, lapwing, curlew, oyster-catcher, sandpiper, redshank and woodcock. Pied flycatcher, redstart and the increasingly rare twite can also be found. Down in the valleys, roe deer can be found grazing woodland edges.

There are far reaching views to the Lakeland fells, to Bowland and to York-shire's Three Peaks. There are also views across the terraces and chimneys of those former mill towns. There are fewer chimneys now and they no longer belch acrid fumes across those towns, but people still escape to these hills and moors as they always have done.

Today the West Pennine Moors is a 90 square mile area of upland moorland, riven with valleys and wooded cloughs. Clough is very much a north country label for a steep sided ravine, often wooded, through which a stream or beck flows. It also became a popular surname in Lancashire.

The view from Winter Hill to Jubilee Tower on Darwen Moor and beyond to Pendle Hill and Yorkshire's Three Peaks.

Pike Stones, a chambered long cairn on Anglezarke Moor.

The landscape is dotted with reservoirs, large and small, that feed the towns and villages that have sprung up in the valleys. There are barely any settlements on the high ground, swept as it is by the prevailing westerly winds that race in off the Irish Sea, but there are historic villages to be found in the valleys and around the edges. This is the first high ground that weather fronts from the west meet and that is why the city corporations built their reservoirs here as the clouds broke on a landscape that gets more than average rainfall each year.

That climate was also ideal for keeping cotton moist; making it easier to work and it is no accident that cotton and textile industries developed around this landscape in the industrial towns of Bolton, Bury, Blackburn, Chorley, Horwich, Accrington, Darwen and Rawtenstall. The mills and chimneys can still be seen from the high moors, but they are largely silent now and many of these buildings have been given over to alternative uses.

The canals and railways followed and threaded their way through the valleys from north to south serving these new industries and the people that made those towns and cities their new home.

Before the Industrial Revolution gathered pace in the towns and villages around this landscape, it was also dotted with more ancient architecture. If you know where to look, you can find old stone circles, burial chambers, round barrows, ancient terraced fields and the remains of a Roman Road. This tells us that the high ground was occupied certainly as far back as the Bronze Age and potentially earlier still to the late Stone Age.

Today this landscape is popular walking country, with footpaths and bridle-ways generally well maintained and clearly signed. Some attractive additions to the scene include the signposts erected by the Peak District & Northern Counties Footpath Society. Many of these date to the 1960s, though more recent examples can also be found across the landscape. This organization dates back to 1894 and is dedicated to defending walker's right of way. It is perhaps fitting that their signs can be found all across this landscape given the local campaigns in 1896 to open up access for all onto Winter Hill and Darwen Moor.

Today there is a wealth of footpaths criss-crossing this landscape and a number of long distance paths stride out across the moors and hills, including the Witton Weaver's Way, the Rossendale Way, the West Pennine Way, the Rotary Way and the Pendle Way.

The Pendle Way encircles the borough of Pendle. It was officially opened in 1987. The circuit is 45 miles, and according to the Long Distance Walkers Association involves 6033 feet of ascent reaching 1827 feet maximum height on Pendle Hill. Its attractions include historical associations with the seventeenth-century Pendle Witches, connections with the Brontës, stone-built villages in the traditional style of East Lancashire and the South Pennines, relics of the weaving and lead mining industries, limestone meadows and millstone grit moorland culminating in the ascent of Pendle Hill.

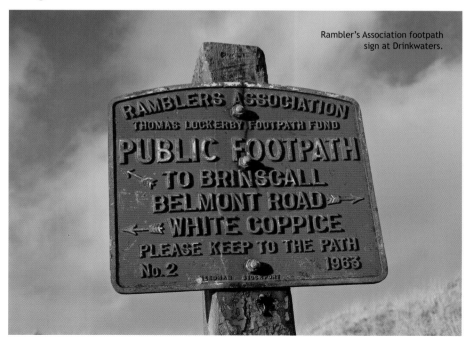

Rambler's Association footpath sign at Drinkwaters.

The Rossendale Way encircles the boundary of Rossendale and was opened in 1985. This circuit is also 45 miles long. The Witton Weaver's Way is a 32 mile long distance path and is perhaps the best introduction to the West Pennine Moors. It explores Lancashire's history, passing weavers cottages, Tudor halls, Victorian estates, historic villages and even Roman Roads. This industrial, agricultural and religious history is complemented by surprisingly beautiful scenery. Unusually for a long distance path, the Way is a network of four circular routes (named the Beamer's, Reeler's, Tackler's and Warper's Trails, respectively 6, 8, 11 and 9 miles), linked together with further sections of trail to form a large loop to the west of Blackburn and Darwen. The route takes in Abbey Village, Darwen Moor and Jumbles Reservoir on the northern outskirts of Bolton. There is a link into Darwen itself.

The Rotary Way follows the borough boundary of Bolton and crosses the West Pennine Moors over Winter Hill, across Cheetham Close and Affetside. It was developed in 2005 to celebrate the centenary of the founding of the Rotary Club.

The West Pennine Way is a 46 mile long distance footpath developed by the Greenmount Community Walking Group to showcase the West Pennine landscape. The route includes a 15 mile link path to the Pennine Way itself.

Jubilee Tower on Darwen Moor.

This wealth of long distance paths illustrates just how popular this part of Lancashire is for walking. This is in part because these hills and heights can be seen from the houses, offices and factories of the towns and cities down in the surrounding valleys. For those working through the week, the pull of those hills and moors has always been strong, symbolising an escape from the mundanity of life for those in search of another day of freedom on the hills. Ewan MacColl, Salford's most famous folk songwriter, composed his classic 'Manchester Rambler' in honour of those who fought for access on Kinder Scout, but in essence he might as well have been singing about these hills above Manchester's mill-towns.

Spring lambs at dusk above Downham village.

This is also a farming landscape. Although the moorland climate can be wet and harsh with poor acidic soils due to the underlying peat on gritstone geology, farming has been an important way of life here. This has predominantly been livestock farming, mainly sheep rearing, with farmers and shepherds supplementing their low income by engaging in other activities such as quarrying.

Fundamentally, the West Pennine Moors is a landscape associated with water. Since the Industrial Revolution, the city fathers of Liverpool, Wigan, Chorley and Bolton understood that this upland landscape could be a gathering ground for the supply of water needed for these growing industrial towns. High rainfall, brought in on the prevailing westerly wind, the impermeable gritstone and the many cloughs, becks, rivers and streams, were the ideal ingredients for collecting water. When dammed, the reservoirs quickly filled and many are now quite naturalised.

This landscape has therefore long been in the care of the water authorities, from the City Corporations, to the North West Water Authority, through to United Utilities today.

Further north lies Pendle Witch Country below Lancashire's most famous hill. Pendle Hill sits alone in the landscape and when seen from the north, east and south is a clear landmark, sitting high and proud above the fields and farms it shelters.

However, Pendle Hill is famous – or should that be infamous – for the events that happened in the early seventeenth century. In 1612 twelve women and men from farmsteads and villages around the foot of Pendle Hill were arrested for practising witchcraft. They were marched across country to be put on trial at Lancaster where nine were sentenced to death. The news spread rapidly across the country and the Pendle Witches tale became the stuff of myth and legend as the truth was exaggerated and the facts of the story became diluted over distance and time.

There are two sides to Pendle Hill – the gentle, pastoral landscape that rolls towards the River Ribble, embracing Downham, Whalley and Clitheroe – and Witch Country – an altogether rougher side to Pendle, sheltered below its south-eastern flanks.

In contrast to the West Pennine Moors, the landscape around Pendle Hill is an altogether more gentle landscape of farmsteads, lush pastures where sheep and

Northbound Fellsman passes Newsholme with a backdrop of Pendle Hill.

Pendle Hill from Downham.

dairy cows graze, with hedgerows and pretty villages. The top of Pendle Hill and the moors that sweep away westwards from the summit are a little wilder. Pendle Hill falls within the Forest of Bowland Area of Outstanding Natural Beauty (AONB), though in many respects it sits apart from the Bowland Fells, separated by the River Ribble and a good few miles of open country. Its designation as an AONB came in 1964.

This has been an inspirational landscape, where George Fox had his vision that led to his foundation of the Quaker movement. This is a landscape rich in history, and not just because of the events around the Pendle Witch trials in 1612, but there are castles, such as that at Clitheroe and the remains of ancient abbeys at Sawley and Whalley.

Pendle Hill is considered by many to be the inspiration for J.R.R.Tolkein's Lonely Mountain in his epic trilogy *Lord of the Rings*. Tolkein stayed at nearby Stoneyhurst College in the 1940s and drew on much of the landscape around the Ribble for inspiration for his books.

The area is well covered by the Ordnance Survey maps and the Explorer 1:25000 scale maps are highly recommended as they provide a wealth of detail to ease navigation for either the suggested short walks at the end of each chapter or for those seeking out their own adventure.

Chris Gee
York, 2017

13

Cricket match underway on the pitch at White Coppice, perhaps the most attractive pitch in the country. The hill behind is The Lowe.

Rivington Pike.

CHAPTER 1

LANCASHIRE'S LAKE DISTRICT

Our adventure begins around Lancashire's "Lake District", a string of reservoirs, now quite naturalised, but still a source of water for Liverpool. There are five main reservoirs in the chain and the landscape is therefore a very popular walking area complemented by attractive villages at White Coppice and Rivington, with Winter Hill and Rivington Pike watching over the scene.

The Rivington area was dramatically changed by the construction of the Anglezarke, Upper Rivington, Lower Rivington and Yarrow Reservoirs which were built to provide Liverpool with a safe, clean water supply. Nine properties in the valley were demolished before construction work began. The Rivington Pike Scheme, still in use today, was undertaken by Thomas Hawksley between 1850 and 1857. The scheme was to construct five reservoirs and a water treatment works at the south end of Lower Rivington with a 17-mile (27 km) pipeline to storage reservoirs at Prescot. Water from two higher level reservoirs, Rake Brook and Lower Roddlesworth, was carried south in The Goit, a man-made channel connecting them to the lower reservoirs. The scheme was expanded in 1856, to include High Bullough Reservoir, built in 1850 by J. F. Bateman to supply water to Chorley. The scheme was further expanded by the construction of the Upper Roddlesworth Reservoir in 1867–75 by Thomas Duncan and Joseph Jackson. The Rivington watershed comprises of 10,000 acres. Yarrow Reservoir, on which work began in 1867, was designed by Thomas Duncan, the Liverpool Borough Engineer.

Looking to distant Redmonds Edge and Spitlers Edge across Yarrow Reservoir and Alance Bridge.

In 1900 Liverpool Corporation attempted to acquire the entire area to safeguard its water supply, and proposed to demolish the entire village. Some buildings were protected and others left vulnerable in an Act of Parliament known as the Liverpool Corporation Act 1902. The Act allowed the Corporation to acquire by compulsory purchase properties in the west of the village, including the Black-a-Moors Head public house (known locally as the 'Black Lad') and New Hall, which were demolished between 1902 and 1905. The result was the small settlement that has remained largely unchanged since then.

The surrounding moors then, as now, also came into the ownership of Liverpool Corporation as they were the gathering grounds for the water that fed the reservoirs.

Today they are a playground for the residents of Bolton, Horwich and Chorley, easily accessible from those towns and yet a world away. As well as being great walking country, they are popular for fishing and boating.

Perhaps the most popular are the Lower and Upper Rivington Reservoirs. The area around Rivington is a real honeypot. The cruck barn at Great House Barn will be busy with families and day-trippers on any given sunny weekend. There is a popular tea room here and Rivington makes an excellent base for exploring the local countryside. It is also home to the West Pennine Moors Countryside Information Centre where a selection of maps, walking books and guide books can be found.

Heapey Waterman's Cottage, Anglezarke Reservoir.
Inset: Great House Barn, Rivington.

Rivington doorways.

Rivington Hall Barn.

The cruck barns at Great House and Rivington Hall are certainly very old, though how old remains unclear. Some historians speculate that they date from Saxon times as there are buildings of a very similar design and construction in Scandinavia that date from before the eleventh century. However, most of the current structures date from the early eighteenth century, though as with many buildings in the area, they have been altered and rebuilt several times over the centuries. Only the crucks, their stone bases and some longitudinal beams (purlins) are original. Both barns were restored by Lord Leverhulme in the very early twentieth century and much altered. This was before listed building status existed and planning regulations were not as strict as they are today. Both Great House Barn and Rivington Hall Barn were used to stable livestock and their feed and in later times were used to store hay through the autumn and winter months. Through the Second World War rationed sugar was stored in Great House Barn. Both barns have been Grade I listed since 1952.

The West Pennine Moors Countryside Information Centre is on the upper floor of Great House, another ancient farm first mentioned in the thirteenth century, though the current building is almost certainly seventeenth century.

Rivington Country Park embraces the landscaped estate of Lord Lever. Before that it was the ancestral home of the de Rivington family. By 1900 the estate had passed into the hands of William Hesketh Lever, the soap baron. Lever owned soap factories at Port Sunlight and was a famous philanthropist, being responsible for the innovative village at Port Sunlight. Lever later became Lord Leverhulme and was responsible for creating the terraced gardens on the slopes below Rivington Pike and Lever Park on the shore of Lower Rivington Reservoir. It was a mark of his philanthropy that he gave Lever Park to the citizens of Bolton in 1902.

Autumn is a particularly rewarding time to come when the wooded terraces below Rivington Pike display a broad spectrum of autumn colours. There are examples of lots of different native and non-native trees throughout the arboretum laid out at Lever Park.

The Pigeon Tower was built in 1910 by Lord Leverhulme as part of his Rivington estate in Lever Park and stands at the north-west edge of the Terraced Gardens. The tower is built in gritstone with three storeys, each a single room. It has a steeply-pitched roof and a corbelled chimney. On the west side is a semi-circular stair turret with a conical roof. The third storey, a sitting room and Lady Lever's sewing/music room, has four-light mullioned windows on two sides giving views of the boating lake. The other two storeys are a dovecote and when in use housed ornamental doves and pigeons. On the west wall are square pigeon holes with perching ledges.

The three floors are linked by a solid stone staircase that runs up the semi-circular spine of the building. Over recent years the Tower has been renovated with its floors repaired in 1974, and its roof replaced in 2005. Today the Tower marks a popular out-and-back circuit for families from the Great House Barn down by Lower Rivington Reservoir.

Rivington Woods in autumn.

Rivington Pike is another popular local landmark and again a focal point for many families climbing up from their cars down below in the country park. At 1187 feet, it is also the destination for a regular fell race from Horwich. This fell race was established by the Lancashire & Yorkshire Railway in 1892. They owned the locomotive and carriage works in nearby Horwich. The people of Bolton and Horwich traditionally climb up here on Good Friday, a remnant of the once popular Pike Fair which took place across Easter. The stone tower that marks the top of the pike was built in 1733 by John Andrews. Andrews was the Lord of the Manor of Rivington at that time. The tower was once used to shelter shooting parties from the prevailing weather and had a wooden roof and windows on all four sides. Despite the threat of demolition in the 1960s, it is now secured as a Grade II listed building. Rivington Pike was also gifted to the people of Bolton in 1902 by Lord Leverhulme, by which time use of the moor for grouse shooting had been stopped by Leverhulme.

Rivington Pike.

Rivington Pike was one of a chain of beacons along the western fells and hills of Lancashire. These were established around 1139 by Ranulph de Blundeville, Earl of Chester. Beacon Fell on the edge of the Bowland Fells took its name in honour of the duty it performed. These beacons were lit to send rapid signals up and down the country in the event of national danger and it was lit on 19 July 1588 during the threat of invasion that came with the Spanish Armada. The beacons could send messages far more quickly than a despatcher on horseback could achieve. It was reputed to be last lit to mark the armistice at the end of the First World War on 11 November 1918.

The Terraced Gardens that descend from Rivington Pike to Rivington Hall are perhaps the most remarkable feature of this landscape. Today they have all the atmosphere of a lost world, a forgotten civilization where nature is rapidly reclaiming grand structures that were built by man in another time. Most of the gardens were laid out in the early years of the twentieth century. Lord Leverhulme was a visionary and created Japanese gardens and terraces, pagodas and artificial waterfalls, including Romanesque Seven Arches Bridge, carriage drives, staircases and an elaborate ballroom known as The Bungalow with a chequer tiled floor. The gardens were still being developed upon his death in 1925. Unfortunately Lever's vision was never fully realized and the gardens became abandoned and overgrown, particularly once the land here was taken over by Liverpool Corporation who owned the reservoirs down in the valley. From the 1970s, some restoration work was carried out under the stewardship of North West Water (now United Utilities) who still own much of the land around here and with the support and manpower of the British Trust for Conservation Volunteers.

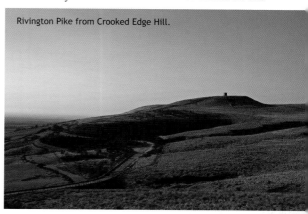

Rivington Pike from Crooked Edge Hill.

Terraced Gardens, Rivington Woods.

21

Rivington Hall is a very attractive hall with a Georgian red brick façade. The hall dates from the 1780s and is on the site of a much older building. The original Rivington Hall was a medieval building of timber frame construction filled with wattle and daub. It was certainly enlarged in 1478 by the Pilkington family who were Lords of the Manor for over four centuries. It was subsequently sold in 1617 to the Breres family who spent years improving the hall, rebuilding much of the property in stone and adding wings in 1694 and 1700 which stand behind the Georgian façade that is seen today. This façade was added in the early 1780s and at the same time much of the medieval core of the hall was demolished as the programme of rebuilding continued.

There was once a water wheel for grinding corn and churning butter alongside Rivington Hall, but this fell into disuse in the very early twentieth century.

Just along the road is the pretty little hamlet of Rivington village, laid out beside a village green complete with stocks. There have been settlements around Rivington for a very long time and the name Rivington is thought to derive either from "a settlement in the rowans" or "a rough farmstead". The settlement is thought to at least date back to Anglo-Saxon times. Through the fourteenth century it was recorded as *Rouyngton* and *Revyngton* and by 1600 had evolved more closely to its current name as *Rovington* and *Ryvington*.

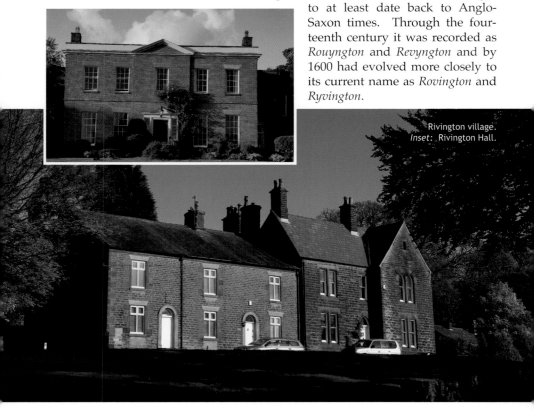

Rivington village.
Inset: Rivington Hall.

The old post office and old school house are particularly attractive. There is a neat little Unitarian chapel which dates from 1703, behind which is a nice tea room. This was the first nonconformist place of worship in Lancashire, founded in 1662, after which followed the Wesley and Methodist movement. After the English Civil War and the Restoration of Charles II in 1662, the clergyman Samuel Newton was expelled from the Church for

Rivington Unitarian chapel.

refusing to accept the Book of Common Prayer and he and his followers went on to erect this Unitarian chapel. The chapel has remained largely unchanged throughout the centuries and still retains its box pews and pulpit. Curiously the chapel and the chapel house behind were frequented by followers of the nine-teenth century American poet Walt Whitman. They were known as the 'Eagle Street College'.

The village is also home to a popular school, once a grammar school estab-lished in 1566 by James Pilkington, Bishop of Durham, though the current build-ing dates to 1714 and is now in use as a primary school.

There was once a temperance hotel in the village, another indicator of the non-conformist tendencies around this corner of Lancashire. By the twentieth century the hotel had become home to the Reverend Fisher who was Vicar in the parish for fifty years. Today the former hotel is known as Fisher House and presents a strik-ing white-painted Georgian front.

Mill Hill handloom weavers' cottages, Rivington.

Rivington village stocks.

Mill Hill Cottages which date to 1788 were home to handloom weavers. The windows in the upper storey are typical of the period, with three sections to allow maximum light onto the upper floor. Another set of handloom weavers' cottages called Pall Mall Cottages can be found further along the road.

The sixteenth-century church stands nearby and Saxon remains have been found in the churchyard. Unusually it has no patron saint. In the past it has been known as St Lawrence, St George, Holy Trinity and St Catherine, but at the current time, this simple 1540 built church is just known as Rivington church.

The village is clustered around a neat little village green complete with stocks, typical of those villages with Anglo-Saxon heritage where the green would once have been common land for grazing. Today Rivington is an enviable place to live either in retirement or as a commuter, but at one time it was home to farmers and handloom weavers.

A particular feature of the area is that almost every farm and cottage has a name associated with a former tenant or owner of the property.

On the eastern shore of Lower Rivington Reservoir on a small promontory known as Coblowe stands an atmospheric ruin of a castle. This is no ancient defensive castle, but a folly, a replica of Liverpool Castle built by Lord Lever-hulme, designed to reflect the original castle as it was just after the English Civil War in 1650 and before its demolition in 1725.

Liverpool Castle, Lever Park.

Liverpool Castle, Lever Park.

Lord Leverhulme was an enthusiastic landscape architect and the replica of Liverpool Castle complemented his terraced gardens and Lever Park. Work on the replica started in 1912 and was part-completed in 1916. The intention was always to create a ruin, rather than a complete replica, but progress slowed and after Leverhulme's death in 1925 work stopped altogether, emphasising the ruined aspect of the castle. Liverpool Castle was in part chosen because the reservoirs were owned by Liverpool Corporation and Leverhulme wanted to acknowledge the connections between Rivington and Liverpool.

The crowds will be spending their time around Rivington, but the connoisseur will seek out Anglezarke Reservoir. This is an altogether quieter part of the world and the circuit of the reservoir is a delight, particularly in late spring when the gorse bushes that surround the reservoir are in flower and the bright yellow flowers emit a strong coconut scent. There is a delightful old waterside house built by Liverpool Corporation in the mid-nineteenth century, known as Waterman's Cottage.

Heapey Waterman's Cottage.

Not far away is the pretty little hamlet of White Coppice with whitewashed cottages and perhaps one of the most attractive cricket grounds in Lancashire, set against a backdrop of The Lowe. It is tucked away at the end of a quiet no through road and it is this remote setting which makes it a lovely place to explore, free of traffic and dotted with those lovely cottages with well-maintained gardens. It's a much sought after place to live these days, but in Victorian times, this was a place of industry and these cottages were home to the lead miners who worked the seams on the moors and factory workers and millworkers who laboured in nearby Chorley.

Stronstrey Bank is a gritstone outcrop that overlooks The Goit – a watercourse that feeds Anglezarke Reservoir. It was built to carry water from the string of reservoirs around Roddlesworth and runs for 4 miles to top up Anglezarke Reservoir.

Gritstone was a much sought after resource and close to the reservoirs can be found the abandoned quarries where gritstone was worked to provide stone for the dams, causeways and reservoir lining. These quarries were largely abandoned in the 1920s and are fast being reclaimed by nature.

White Coppice and The Lowe.
Inset: Stronstrey Bank from The Goit.

SUGGESTED SHORT WALKS

Anglezarke Reservoir   (4 miles / 6.4 km)

This is a simple circuit of Anglezarke
Reservoir, one of the quieter corners of
Lancashire's Lake District affording good
views of Rivington Pike and Winter Hill.

Winter Hill from above
Anglezarke Reservoir.

The walk starts in Leicester Mill Quarry
car park on the eastern shore of Anglezarke Reservoir.

From the car park entrance the way
heads through a kissing gate to join the
surfaced path that runs north alongside
the reservoir. This runs on through trees,
but maintains good views across Angle-
zarke Reservoir. Heading east beside a small inlet the path splits to run alongside
the western edge of High Bullough Reservoir, a tiny companion to its much larger
Anglezarke brother.

A helpful information board gives an indication of some of the birdlife that is
likely to be seen or at least your soundtrack on this walk through this wooded
corner. Great spotted woodpeckers can often be heard drumming in the woods.

Beyond High Bullough Reservoir and below Spen Cob the path emerges from
trees into more open country dotted with gorse bushes which will be displaying
their bright yellow flowers in spring and summer and giving off a heady coconut
scent. Up above is Anglezarke Moor with its Bronze Age relics.

Anglezarke Reservoir from Grey Heights.

Bluebells in the woods below Stronstrey Bank.
Inset: Whitewashed cottages, White Coppice.

The path continues back into trees alongside the reservoir and runs on to join Moor Road where we turn left to cross the outfall of The Goit into Anglezarke reservoir. A highly recommended diversion runs alongside The Goit below Stronstrey Bank to the attractive hamlet of White Coppice. It is a simple out and back stroll and route finding couldn't be easier, The Goit will lead you all the way there and back again to this point.

Meanwhile Moor Road runs past Heapey Waterman's Cottage, a timber-framed black and white building that is better seen once we are back beside the reservoir. Where the road swings sharp right, a footpath runs left back alongside the reservoir below Grey Heights Wood. This path runs on through the trees to join Heapey Fold Lane. Turning left on this stony track, this runs a straight course parallel with the reservoir and offering good views across to Winter Hill.

Heapey Fold Lane swings right at Kay's Farm to join Charnock Back Lane where you turn left to follow this below the grassy embankment of the reservoir. Just before the embankment runs out and the road bends right a little, a path on the left runs back towards the reservoir and follows the shore round to rejoin the road that crosses the dam that separates Anglezarke Reservoir from Upper Rivington Reservoir. Turning left onto this road and crossing the dam, stay with the road as it swings left and at a T junction turn left to stay with the shoreline path back to Leicester Mill Quarry car park.

Rivington Pike and Country Park   (2¾ miles / 4.5 km)

Appreciation of this walk can be greatly enhanced by purchasing a copy of the Trail Guide from the Great House Visitor Information Centre. The guide provides a wealth of detail on the features that will be encountered on the walk.

Starting from Great House Barn car park, cross the road and take the long drive to Rivington Hall directly ahead. Continue past Rivington Hall and Barn to South Lodge through a stand of beech trees and take the path that climbs to a junction where you bear right. Above you are the terraces created by Leverhulme and below one of the many garden shelters.

Archway, Terraced Gardens, Rivington Woods.

The trail continues to a stone footbridge over the Ravine. This series of cascades is completely man made, but over the years has become very naturalised. Crossing the bridge the trail takes the steps to the left and continues on to Roynton Lane. Turn up stone steps to enter the Japanese Water Gardens with the remains of an ornamental lantern base on the left. Rounding a corner the main garden and lake are on the right hand side.

Continue on the footpath up the steps away from the lake and towards a small group of ruined buildings. These are the remains of the bothy, tool and potting sheds, the storeshed and a small stable. Continue on this path to pass the partly walled Kitchen Gardens and past the remains of the Fernery, boiler room and garage.

Bungalow ballroom site, Terraced Gardens, Rivington Woods.

Seven Arch Bridge, Terraced Gardens, Rivington Woods.

The trail continues to the site of the Stone House whose rounded stone pillars remain. The trail climbs the Long Walk, a long flight of steps that leads through a stone arch-way. To the left was once the Great Lawn, but our way heads right to the site of the Tennis Court. From above the Tennis Court shelter take a path to the left which cuts across Long Walk and heads on up to the terrace known as Lever's Walk. Climb the steps further to turn left onto the large levelled area of the Bungalow Ballroom site. Evidence of the chequer tiled floor can still be found together with the faint outline of the circular ballroom.

Continue along the broad track to pass the site of Belmont Lodge. Ahead is the distinctive Pigeon Tower. Descend past the Swimming Pool to take the first path on the right and drop via the garden shelter steps to Seven Arch Bridge, built in 1910 to a Romanesque design.

Cross the bridge and head down the stepped path to rejoin the main track close to South Lodge. Retrace your steps to South Lodge, Rivington Hall and back to Great House Barn.

Pigeon Tower above Rivington Woods.

Rivington Pike. *Below:* The Pigeon Tower and Rivington Woods seen from Lever Park in Autumn.

CHAPTER 2

BOLTON'S MOORS

Belmont village and reservoir and beyond Darwen Moor, seen from Grange Brow on the slopes of Winter Hill.

Below: Cheetham Close and the north-west suburbs of Bolton, seen from Grange Brow on the lower slopes of Winter Hill.

Winter Hill dominates the landscape around Bolton, Horwich and Chorley. For many Lancastrians, whether they are returning from the north or the south, the distinctive outline of Winter Hill with its towering transmission tower is a clear indication that they are nearly home. Winter Hill is one of the highest points in the West Pennine Moors. The Ordnance Survey column marks the summit at 1496 feet (456 metres). It is further enhanced by a towering 1000 foot (300 metre) television transmitter mast, securely held in place by steel ropes. The summit is also home to other telecommunications paraphernalia.

The current mast dates from 1966 and replaced an earlier mast erected in 1956. Remarkably there is a lift inside the main column to give access to the top of the mast.

It was a wise place to choose because on a clear day the summit of Winter Hill offers views to the Yorkshire Dales, the Lake District Fells and the high peaks of Snowdonia, as well as those hills and fells that are within Lancashire – the Bowland Fells and Pendle Hill being the most obvious. It is also possible to see Blackpool Tower from here. The hill is well named, because it can often lie under a blanket of snow during harsher winters.

This is a landscape that has a human past. From Neolithic times, man made his mark up here and it's possible to seek out the impressions early man made on this high ground. There is an old cairn on Noon Hill on Rivington Moor. This burial cairn is thought to be of Bronze Age origin which makes it over 3000 years old. When excavated in 1958 by Bolton Archaeological Society, it revealed the remains of two humans and a broken urn which is now on display in Bolton Museum. Arrowheads, the remains of a flint knife and scrapers were also found.

Winter Hill from Anglezarke Moor.
Inset: Winter Hill and its telecommunications masts seen from the Bronze Age cairn on Noon Hill.

Pike Stones chambered long cairn on Anglezarke Moor.

Pike Stones – a chambered long cairn – looks out to Chorley from the western edge of Anglezarke Moor. It consisted of one burial chamber constructed of large upright slabs, capped by two lintel slabs, covered by a huge mound of stones and turf. The cairn was aligned almost exactly north-south, with the burial chamber under the wider northern end.

Today the cairn has been badly robbed and the main features are the five large gritstone slabs, the remains of the burial chamber.

Surprisingly, evidence suggests that the bodies were not interred directly in the tomb, but were left outside, perhaps at the entrance to the cairn, for birds and wild animals to consume the flesh and then, probably after elaborate ceremonies, the bones were placed inside the chamber.

Pike Stones is the earliest man-made structure in the area and only one other chambered tomb has been found in Lancashire. The monument must have taken an immense amount of labour to construct and like most long barrows was erected in a prominent position, located on a ridge at a height of just over 900 feet (276 metres). This gave the Neolithic builders excellent views, and made the structure visible from a wide area of the Lancashire plain, perhaps warning other people that the land belonged to the builders.

Winter Hill in winter, seen from Top of Turton.

Round Loaf is an old burial cairn, covered in earth and sits high on Anglezarke Moor. Archaeologists have struggled to date it; it could be either Bronze Age or older still from the Neolithic Age or Stone Age. It displays all the attributes of a Bronze Age round barrow, but it is unusually large and one of the largest in North West England. If it is Bronze Age, that would make it nearly 3500 years old. It is certainly unmistakeable and clearly man made, sitting proud of the surrounding moorland. The cairn on the top is from more recent times and marks it as a place of pilgrimage for modern day walkers. Nearby is Devil's Ditch which is also thought to date back to the same time as Round Loaf. It runs for a short distance in a straight line with no obvious purpose.

Lead was discovered here in Roman times and lead miners came to work the veins of lead around Lead Mines Clough on the lower slopes of Anglezarke Moor. It wasn't a particularly productive source of lead and the workings here went through boom and bust years. The 1780s were the most successful and by 1837 all working of lead here had ceased. Nearly 150 years later the site was excavated by the British Trust for Conservation Volunteers and this work included the construction of a trail to explore the workings, dotted with helpful interpretation boards. The most interesting remains include a slime pit where water containing lead particles was stored to allow the lead to settle. This silt that formed was full of lead and was therefore dug out once the water had been drained off. A sough carried the water from the lead workings. There are also the remains of a pumping shaft and waterwheel pit. Water was carried from a spring along a wooden trestle aqueduct to drive the waterwheel. The wooden structure is long gone, but two stone supporting pillars remain. Nature has rapidly recolonized this old industrial landscape and a visit in June can reveal a wealth of wildflowers, including common spotted orchids.

Round Loaf burial cairn on Anglezarke Moor.

Later came the coalminers who dug scrapes in the ground to mine the coal seams that outcropped on Winter Hill. The clues are still there in some of the names on the map: Colliers Row Road near Smithills Dean, Coal Pit Lane which runs onto Winter Hill and Burnt Edge Colliery. A scan of the Ordnance Survey map will reveal more clues: disused shafts and mine levels marked across the landscape. The coal was generally of a poor quality and so later deep shafts were never built, but it was of enough calorific value to power some of the early, local steam engines.

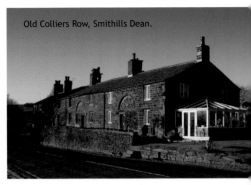
Old Colliers Row, Smithills Dean.

This landscape has also been quarried for gritstone. Delf and delph, a local name for a quarry, appears regularly on maps.

With industrialization came the Victorian landowners and these high moors became grouse moors, barred to the working classes. Heather flourished and grouse butts were built. Gamekeepers were brought in and wildlife was managed. Though long redundant, some grouse butts still stand today in places, though this landscape is now open to all.

In September 1896, Winter Hill was the scene of a mass trespass long before that iconic event on Kinder Scout in 1932. In late Victorian times, these upland moors were the preserve of the landowners for their sport of grouse shooting. Winter Hill was owned by Colonel Ainsworth who lived at Smithills Hall. For the Glorious Twelfth in 1896, Ainsworth decided to close the moors, erecting a gate across Coalpit Lane and raising prominent 'Private' signs. Up until that point, people from Bolton had had the opportunity to climb up to these heights.

Left: Winter Hill and its telecommunications masts seen from Rivington Pike.
Right: On the summit of Winter Hill amongst the masts.

Dean Black Brook below Drinkwaters looking on to Great Hill.

Below: Winter Hill from Great Hill in winter.

The closure sparked anger and uproar in Bolton and by September a group of 8000 protesters – led by the Bolton Socialist Party – had gathered to undertake a mass trespass on Winter Hill and insist on their right to access the moors and hills around the town where they lived and worked. The protestors made their way from Barrow Bridge across Smithills Moor along Coalpit Lane to Winter Hill. A group of gamekeepers and police officers met them at a gate onto the moor, but the sheer volume of numbers overwhelmed the keepers and officers and the protestors marched on to Winter Hill and then down into Belmont. A week later, a further group of about 12,000 protesters made the same journey. The action inspired a local dialect poet – Allen Clarke who wrote under the pen name Teddy Ashton – to compose a verse he called 'The Battle for Winter Hill'.

It was a short lived victory as by mid-September, Colonel Ainsworth began legal proceedings against the organizers of the protests and by early 1897, ten of these were on trial at Manchester Chancery Court. Although numerous witnesses came forth with evidence that Coalpit Lane had a long history of access onto Winter Hill, the landowner won the case.

Before the Countryside and Rights of Way Act in 2004 came into being, local ramblers had since 1996 enjoyed access to these upland heights thanks to the enlightened approach of the local authorities who negotiated access with the local landowners. A stone at the gate on Coalpit Lane commemorates the events of 1896.

Winter Hill and Noon Hill from Sparks Bridge.

Two Lads on Winter Hill looking to Bolton and Manchester.

Winter Hill has also been a place of tragedy. Look closely on the map and you'll spot Two Lads which on the ground appear as a group of stones. These two memorial cairns on the hill are also known as *Wilder Lads*. There are differing opinions on why they were erected. Details of the site were recorded in 1776 and 1883. Thomas Hampson in 1883 described 'Two Lads' as the graves of two chil-

dren of a Saxon king, Edgar and recorded that Winter Hill was previously known as Edgar Hill. The cairns could mark the site on which two boys lost their way on the moor and died of exposure in a snow-storm.

Scotsman's Stump marks the spot where a gruesome murder took place. George Henderson, a pedlar from Scotland was making his way across the moor on 9 November 1838 when he was shot. The following year, James Whittle, a collier from Belmont was charged with his murder having been seen on the

Memorial to the crew of a crashed Wellington bomber, Lead Mines Clough.

moors with a gun. Whittle was later acquitted at Liverpool Crown Court and found not guilty and the case remains unsolved.

Just above Lead Mines Clough there is a memorial to the six aircrew who lost their lives on 12 November 1943 when the Wellington bomber they were flying on a training mission crashed into Hurst Hill on Anglezarke Moor. On 27 February 1958 a flight from Douglas on the Isle of Man to Ringway Airport in Manchester crashed into Winter Hill during heavy fog and snow with the loss of over 30 lives. Remarkably seven people survived the crash. The disaster is marked by a plaque on the side of one of the telecommunications buildings on the summit.

Other air crashes on Winter Hill include a two seater aircraft in the 1920s, an American warplane on 7 August 1942, an Airspeed Oxford on 24 December 1943 and several Spitfires, Hurricanes and a Gloster Meteor jet which crashed in 1953. The last recorded aircrash on the hill was in 1968.

The moors of Bolton climb quickly away from the suburbs around Barrow Bridge where there is a country park and Smithills Hall. The high ground then expands across Smithills Moor, over Rivington Moor and Winter Hill to the moors above Belmont.

Barrow Bridge dates from 1846 and was built as a village to serve two spinning mills. Upon closure, the village became deserted as the mills had been the only source of work in the area. As with White Coppice, Barrow Bridge is now a much sought after place to live and the village now falls within a conservation area. The towering Barrow Bridge chimney is now preserved and marks the site of the spinning mills. The village featured in the novel *Coningsby* by one-time Prime Minister Benjamin Disraeli.

Smithills Hall.

Smithills Hall is a well preserved Tudor hall or manor house with a typical black and white façade. It has its origins in the fourteenth century when it was built by William de Ratcliffe as a fortified manor house. The Great Hall dates from this time. There were subsequent extensions, including the East Wing in the time of Henry VIII. The Victorians enthusiastically enlarged the hall, retaining the Tudor style and much of what is typically regarded as the Tudor style actually dates to that Victorian extension. The house later became home to Colonel Ainsworth who we met earlier. In 1938, Bolton Corporation took over the building and surrounding estate and part of the building is now open as a museum. Smithills is a mecca for Boltonians. As well as the hall and the 2000 acre country park, the old coaching house was also a popular dining and entertaining venue throughout the 1970s and 1980s.

Belmont village is a popular commuter village for Bolton, handily placed on

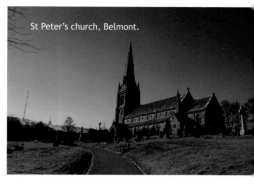

St Peter's church, Belmont.

the main Blackburn Road and served by buses from Bolton along what was once the turnpike road from Bolton to Preston. It is also the earliest recorded settlement in the West Pennine Moors with records showing it was a settlement in 1212. Until 1804 it was known as Hordern and although small, was home to a thriving textile, bleach and dying industry, some of which continues today. The Black Dog is a popular pub dating from the eighteenth century and makes a popular watering hole for those that have undertaken the climb onto Winter Hill. Opposite, a fountain, erected in 1897 to mark the Diamond Jubilee of Queen Victoria sits adjacent to a small green. Belmont Reservoir, built in 1826, has a popular sailing club.

It's a quick climb above Belmont to the moors around Sharples Higher End, Redmond's Edge, Spitler's Edge and Great Hill, then on to Wheelton Moor and Withnell Moor. There are spectacular views from Withnell Moor and Great Hill to the Bowland Fells in North Lancashire, to Pendle Hill and if you're lucky, to the Three Peaks in the Yorkshire Dales, with Ingleborough being instantly recognisable. At 1250 feet, Great Hill is a popular summit and in recent years old flagstones from the floors of redundant textile mills down in the valleys have been brought up onto the moor to help protect the peat surface from erosion caused by the thousands of walking boots that carry their owners up to this heady height. It's worth the climb for the view across to Jubilee Tower on Darwen Moor, Winter Hill and Rivington Pike. It's a great example of recycling and it is perhaps fitting that those great gritstone slabs that once formed the foundations and floors of the mills and factories where so many worked, should now find further use under the boots of the ramblers of today, protecting the heather and peat from erosion so that it can be enjoyed by the ramblers of tomorrow.

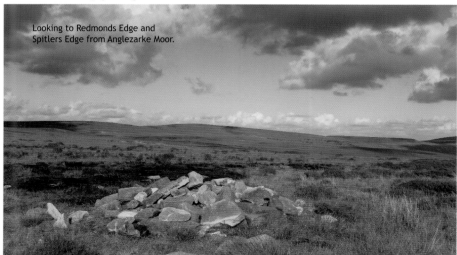

Looking to Redmonds Edge and Spitlers Edge from Anglezarke Moor.

The ruined farmstead at Drinkwater's on Wheelton Moor looking to Great Hill.

These moors are acidic and peaty and while over the centuries, much effort has been invested to graze livestock on the moors, the empty and abandoned farmsteads around Solomon's Temple and Drinkwater's are testament to how difficult it is to make a living farming sheep on these moors. It can be a forlorn landscape – many of the ruined farmsteads are in an advanced state of collapse and the drystone walls are not maintained anymore and have tumbled down in many places. In many ways though it can be a romantic landscape and the ruins make fascinating foreground interest to photographs taken of the surrounding scene. At Drinkwater's Farm, sheltered by a stand of sycamore trees, look out for Joe's Cup, marked by a brass plaque: this is an old well that would once have been a source of drinking water for the farmstead. You will often find a stand of sycamore trees around these old ruined farm buildings, a fast growing tree, they would provide some degree of shelter from the prevailing westerly wind.

The ruined farmstead at Solomon's Temple on Withnell Moor.

SUGGESTED SHORT WALKS

Winter Hill from Belmont   (5½ miles / 8.8 km)

Starting from the Hordern Butts Delf car park on Rivington Road near the head of Ward's Reservoir, a path runs alongside the reservoir to the dam and then along the road to the junction next to the Black Dog public house. Heading across Maria Square, past cottages and a mill pond, the way runs on to turn left on Egerton Road.

Staying with the road past the bleach and dye works, a stile on the right hand side takes you into a field and downhill to a footbridge at the head of Ornamental Reservoir. Take the right hand fork to run on past the sluice gate and above this deep wooded clough. This runs on to Greenhill Farm from where a footpath quickly brings you to the A675.

Crossing over, head through a gate into a plantation of trees and follow the broad path to an old driveway. A good track then begins to climb the lower slopes of Winter Hill towards Grange Brow with Lower Height and Folds Pasture to the left. Crossing a stile continue uphill heading directly for the cluster of telecommunications towers on the summit. Joining a service road a short distance to the right takes you to the summit Ordnance Survey column.

Stay with the fence and then climb a stile in the fence to where the ground quickly drops away to Hordern Stoops. The path runs parallel with the fence helping with route finding as you lose height rapidly down to the Rivington Road at Hordern Stoops. Turn right to follow the road briefly in the Belmont direction before heading left over a stile on a footpath that contours alongside Hoar Stones Brow and Hoar Stones Delf. Reaching an old out building a footpath heads to the right and back to the Rivington Road on the edge of Belmont. The dam of Ward's Reservoir is directly ahead and a waterside path takes you back to the car park at Hordern Butts Delf car park.

Left: Looking down on Cheetham Close and Egerton from Folds Pasture, Winter Hill.
Right: Looking across to Spitlers Edge and Redmonds Edge from Moor Bottom on Winter Hill.

Great Hill and Redmond's Edge from Belmont   (9 miles / 14.5 km)

From Hordern Butts Delf car park just west of Belmont on the Rivington Road, head west along Rivington Road with Hordern or Ward's Brook on your left and Hoar Stones Brow on your right. Continue on the road to the summit at Hordern Stoops where there is a Boundary Stone. From here head directly north beside the wall on the climb across rough pasture to Will Narr on Hordern Pasture.

A straight and grassy path heads west towards Higher Hempshaw's along the top of a low embankment. Continue through crumbling walls past the ruins of Higher Hempshaw's to the ruined farmstead at Lower Hempshaw's. Although the footpath continues across Sam Pasture, the way is indistinct and particularly moist underfoot. A drier and easier alternative is to head north from the ruins of Lower Hempshaw's on the track that runs north outside a plantation to cross a brook.

This joins a track at a T junction where you turn left to head west on this second track to wind down to the farm buildings at Simms. From Simms, rejoin the footpath to continue in a westerly direction above Wilkinson Bullough and at a fork, take the right hand path that drops down into Lead Mines Clough. Crossing a footbridge, climb up the other side to join the bridleway that leads on to Jepson's Gate.

Inset: Redmonds Edge and Spitlers Edge seen from Higher Hempshaw's.

Will Narr seen from Hordern Stoops.

Continue ahead on Moor Road as it winds past Manor House and Spen Cob to continue by Siddlow Fold Farm and then more steeply downhill to where the road meets the top of Anglezarke Reservoir. Turn right through a kissing gate to head along a track. After a stile the track continues on to another kissing gate with the gritstone edge of Stronstrey Bank above and on the right hand side. The track continues parallel with The Goit to the edge of White

Manor House below Anglezarke Moor.

Coppice. It's worth a detour to the left into White Coppice, but our route heads north, climbing a cobbled track to a Peak & Northern Counties Footpath sign that indicates the way to Belmont Road and Brindle.

The path heads due east passing ruined farms as it marches across Anglezarke Moor with Dean Black Brook down below on the left. Continue past Coppice Stile House and Stake to the ruins at Drinkwater's surrounded by sycamore trees. Beyond Drinkwater's, at a fork, take the left hand path above the ruins of Great Hill Farm to begin the obvious climb up onto Great Hill, joining a flagged path for the final few yards. This offers panoramic views all around the West Pennines, to the Bowland Fells and Lakeland.

The flagged path continues away from the summit in a south-easterly direction with the transmitter on Winter Hill as a waymarker. This is moist, peaty moorland, but the flagged path – recovered from old and abandoned Lancashire cotton mills – helps with both route finding and keeping boots dry. The way drops into a dip to cross a stream and then climbs first on to Redmonds Edge and then onto Spitlers Edge, all the while following a crumbling drystone wall that marked the parish boundary. Beyond Higher Anshaw, the path starts its descent towards Hordern Pasture and Will Narr and then down further to Hordern Stoops with Winter Hill directly ahead. Rejoining the Rivington Road, turn left to head back to the car park at Hordern Butts Delf.

Great Hill seen from the ruins of Drinkwater's on Wheelton Moor.

Looking to Winter Hill from Great Hill.

Below: Looking to the distant Jubilee Tower on Darwen Moor from the ruins of Solomon's Temple on Withnell Moor.

CHAPTER 3
DARWEN'S MOORS

Jubilee Tower on Darwen Hill seen from Darwen Moor.

Below: Ling heather in bloom on Darwen Moor.

Jubilee Tower on Darwen Hill looking to the distant Bowland Fells.
Inset: Peak District & Northern Counties footpath signs, Darwen Moor.

Darwen Moor was possibly one of the first open spaces to be granted to the working classes. It became an urban common in 1896 and has been openly accessible to walkers and families climbing up from Darwen. Long before Benny Rothman and colleagues organised the mass trespass onto Kinder Scout in 1932, there was a battle between ramblers and local landowners taking place on the West Pennine Moors. Footpaths and old packhorse routes had criss-crossed these moors for centuries, but as they fell under the ownership of wealthy industrialists who were keen to pursue their shooting interests, some were closed to members of the public.

In 1878, the local Lord of the Manor, the Reverend Duckworth, closed the grouse moor, leading to outrage amongst the citizens of Darwen who had always enjoyed access to these hills and moors. This was at a time of increasing politicisation of the working classes who valued the escape from the industry, smoke and grime of the valleys below. Organised protests, such as the example on nearby Winter Hill, led to a campaign to reinstate access for all. This was over a century before legislation in 2004 finally secured what that campaign had started. The campaign reached the High Court and on 6 September 1896, a civic procession with up to 15,000 people marched onto the moor to celebrate their victory. This procession would inspire a similar campaign in nearby Bolton on the same day. 300 acres of Darwen Moor was established as an urban common and ramblers and red grouse can now roam without fear of the guns.

The moors of Longworth, Turton and Darwen occupy the high ground between the Belmont Road and the Blackburn Road. The old coach road from Bolton to Preston ran below Turton Moor and much of this old carriageway can still be walked today.

This is a wide open landscape and almost always within sight is Jubilee Tower on Darwen Hill as well as Holcombe Moor, Peel Tower, Winter Hill and Great Hill. There are more distant views to Big Grey Stones on Turton Moor and Hog Lowe Pike beyond Holcombe Moor. Hog Lowe Pike presents the characteristic outline of an ancient burial mound, though this isn't confirmed.

Short-eared owls quarter the landscape here in search of voles and mice. In many ways this is now an empty landscape. Farmsteads were abandoned when Liverpool Corporation acquired the high ground as gathering ground for its reservoirs. Whewell's is a good example of one of these abandoned farmsteads. It is named after George Whewell, one of the former occupants. Whewell was an executioner during the English Civil War and apparently one of his victims was the Earl of Derby who was beheaded in Bolton. Whewell's skull is preserved in nearby Affetside and is locally known as the Affetside Skull. Another abandoned farmstead – Stepback Cottage – on Darwen Moor was the scene of a gruesome murder in 1860.

Short-eared owl on Darwen Moor.

Frozen pond on Darwen Moor.

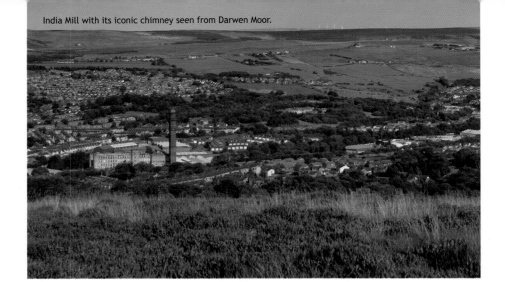

India Mill with its iconic chimney seen from Darwen Moor.

The moors look down on the terraced roofscape of Darwen and its iconic India Mill chimney. The chimneys of Darwen are silent these days and the air is much cleaner now. The India Mill chimney was built in 1867 to serve the textile mill operated by Eccles Shorrock. It was built in the Italianate style of a Venetian bell-tower, though the streets and terraces of Darwen have little in common with Venice, except that they can often be wet! The architect Ernest Bates is said to have used the bell tower that overlooks St Mark's Square in Venice for his inspiration. Local legend has it that when the chimney opened, a celebratory dinner complete with brass band took place on top of the chimney. This seems highly unlikely.

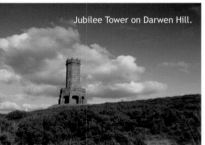

Jubilee Tower on Darwen Hill.

Darwen Moor offers far reaching views to the Bowland Fells and across to nearby Winter Hill. Down below are the small reservoirs of Earnsdale (built in 1854) and Sunnyhurst Hey (built in 1875).

At 1220 feet, Darwen Hill was the obvious place for the construction of yet another tower on top of one of Lancashire's peaks. Jubilee Tower is 86 feet tall and was built between 1897 and 1898 to mark the Diamond Jubilee of Queen Victoria in June of 1897. Or perhaps it was really the people of Darwen celebrating the fact that two years earlier they had secured access to Darwen Moor, as suggested in an anonymous letter to the *Darwen News* that read "a landmark to be seen far and wide, and while commemorating the record year, it would also fulfil a similar function with regard to the celebration of the Freedom of the Darwen Moors." 65 steps lead to a viewing platform that offers distant views to the Lake District Fells, the Bowland Fells and Yorkshire's Three Peaks.

The tower suffered storm damage in 1947 and some years of neglect and vandalism followed, but it was restored and refurbished in 1972.

Not far away is a place marked on the map as Lyon's Den. There is no sign of a building here now, but in the late eighteenth century this was reputed to the home of John Lyon, a 7-foot giant of a man.

Sunnyhurst Wood has its origins as a covert for pheasants and red legged partridge, but in 1902 it was bought by the citizens of Darwen to honour the Coronation of King Edward VII. It is fascinating that so much of the landscape around here, from Rivington Pike, to Lever Park, to Sunnyhurst Wood, should

The Gamekeeper's Cottage, Sunnyhurst Wood.

pass into public ownership around the same time. There is clearly a history of celebration here as the large house that now operates as a tea room was built in 1911 to celebrate the Coronation of King George V. The woodland is also home to a gem of a visitor centre inside the old gamekeeper's cottage. Items of local history are on display here.

Roddlesworth Wood is a popular destination and the springtime visitor will be rewarded with a carpet of bluebells throughout the wood. The route from Ryal Fold follows an old cart road built in the late nineteenth century over which horse-drawn waggons carried coal to the now demolished Hollinshead Mill. This area is criss-crossed with old packhorse trails including Dean Lane which ran from Tockholes to Darwen.

Jubilee Tower on Darwen Hill
seen from Lyon's Den.

Jubilee Tower on Darwen Hill seen from Darwen Golf Club.

Below: Jubilee Tower on heather-clad Darwen Hill.

The River Roddlesworth – also known as Rocky Brook – flows through the heart of the wood. The wood is also home to three reservoirs, built by Liverpool Corporation in the mid-nineteenth century. Liverpool Corporation acquired much of the land around here as gathering ground for its reservoirs. The 4 mile long cut – The Goit – takes excess water down to the reservoir at Anglezarke.

The southern end of the wood hides the ruins of Hollinshead Hall. There has been a manor house on this site since the fourteenth century, although the current ruins date from a much later time. Eccles Shorrock, who owned India Mill in Darwen, was resident for a time, but the house was later abandoned as Liverpool Corporation took over much of this landscape. The ruins have been cleared and made safe and an interpretation board gives an insight into how the house would have been in its heyday.

Within the woods, it is worth seeking out Slipper Lowe, a heathery clearing on high ground within the trees which offers superb views to the Bowland Fells and Pendle Hill.

There is a handy little information centre at Hollinshead Terrace where a row of terraced cottages mark the adjacent site of an old textile mill. This is a popular starting point for walks onto Darwen Moor or down into Roddlesworth Woods and the Royal Arms is an excellent local public house. It is an example of that fast disappearing multi-roomed public house and offers a broad range of real ales, some from the locally famous Thwaite's brewery in Blackburn.

The ruins of Hollinshead Hall.

Earnsdale Reservoir from Darwen Moor.

Abbey Village on the Blackburn Road is a long street village of former mill-worker's terraces and cottages. There was a mill here from 1846 through to 1971 and it was the sole source of employment for the villagers who must now commute to nearby Blackburn or Bolton for work. There are some historic houses in the surrounding area, many dating to the seventeenth century, including Red Lea Farm, Ryal Farm and Chapels Farm. Nearby Tock-holes is a much more scattered village and home to both an old school and Tockholes United Reform church, one of many non-conformist chapels in this part of Lancashire where the spirit of breaking away from the established Church grew strong through the eighteenth and early nineteenth century. Until those first chapels were built in the eighteenth century, non-conformist services were held in secluded spots such as Fairy Battery near Entwistle Reservoir.

Eighteenth-century doorway, Ryal Fold.

54

SUGGESTED SHORT WALKS

Ryal Fold, Darwen Moor and Jubilee Tower (4¾ miles / 7.6 km)

From the car park at Ryal Fold, head past the Royal Arms pub and take a rough track on the right. This runs through the small cluster of buildings at Ryal Fold where you head left into a farmyard. Through a gateway, a track runs into a field heading north before you head in a north-easterly direction on a footpath that runs along the right hand edge of the field to the far corner where you reach a junction of five ways. Here you join an old packhorse route to drop downhill to the dam wall of Earnsdale Reservoir.

Join the Witton Weavers Way to run along the top edge of Sunnyhurst Wood. Stay with the top of the wood until the path begins to drop downhill steeply to the bottom where you encounter a pool and a number of stone arched bridges. Head along to the main driveway through the woods along the valley floor. Turn right on a track that leads in a southerly direction behind Sunnyhurst and the edge of suburban Darwen to the Sunnyhurst public house and a small car park.

Continue on a footpath between buildings to begin the steep climb onto Darwen Moor. Fork right through the heather with the destination of Jubilee Tower very clearly uphill and ahead. However, continue contouring along above Sunnyhurst Hey Reservoir and Higher Wenshead Farm and then double back left along the edge path to the waiting tower.

Head directly south away from the tower on the path across the moor. It swings left to a junction of paths where you turn right to head across the top of the moor to a crossroads of paths. Climbing the stile ahead, continue downhill with the path into Stepback Clough. Passing a ruined building, the path runs down into the clough and crosses Stepback Brook.

A good track now leads out of the trees and through a gate to head diagonally across fields towards the row of cottages at Ryal Fold and the car park.

Jubilee Tower on Darwen Hill seen from Ryal Fold.

55

Turton Moor and Longworth Moor (5½ miles / 8.8 km)

From Crookfield Road car park just off the A675 Belmont Road, return to the road at a sharp bend. A good track – the old coach road – heads in a southerly direction towards Old Man's Hill. However, at the first opportunity on the left, head through a gateway on the Witton Weaver's Way to run along to Higher Pasture Barn Farm.

The path swings left to head towards the lower slopes of Turn Lowe and then swings right, staying with the Witton Weaver's Way towards Green Lowe. Above, unseen on Turton Moor, are the groups of rocks known as Hanging Stones and Big Grey Stones. At a fork, take the right hand path, leaving the Witton Weaver's Way to cross the stream on a footbridge. The path winds on through old coal workings across Cranshaws to a cross-roads of footpaths.

The ruins of Whewell's farmstead, Turton Moor.

Turn right here to head south to the ruins at Whewell's. A single tree stands beside this crumbling farmstead. The way continues in the same direction across the moor. Stay with the path as it contours round to the right around the lower flanks of Turton Moor, a part of the landscape known as Grindle End.

The line of the old tramway on Turton Moor.

Head towards Rabbit Warren where you meet the head of an old tramway. Turn right here on the path as it then swings left to head in a south-westerly direction towards Moor Side on Longworth Moor. At a fork, take the right-hand path to continue contouring below Longworth Moor to a crossroads of paths where you rejoin the Witton Weaver's Way.

Turn right on the old coach road, a good track now and staying with the Witton Weaver's Way as it heads above Higher Pasture House and across the moorland around Pasture Houses Hey. The track runs on by Long Lands to Catherine Edge in a very obvious course that leads to Lower Pasture Barn Farm and skirts Old Man's Hill on the left. Continue in a generally northerly direction on the track as it heads back to join Crookfield Road at a sharp bend where the car park awaits just along to the left.

Jubilee Tower seen from a heather-clad Darwen Moor.

Jubilee Tower at sunset.

Below: The sun sets over Sunnyhurst Hey Reservoir.

CHAPTER 4

A THIRST FOR WALKING: AROUND ENTWISTLE

Hall i'th'Wood.

Below: Beehive coke ovens at Broadhead.

Entwistle is a popular walking base, helped no doubt by easy access by road and a railway station and the popular Strawbury Duck pub. Eighteenth-century New Hall is an attractive local feature. Another string of reservoirs: Turton & Entwistle, Wayoh and Jumbles make this a very popular weekend retreat for the residents of Bolton and Darwen.

Turton and Entwistle Reservoir was built between 1831 and 1840. When Entwistle Dam was built in 1832, it was the highest dam wall in England. The dam was designed by Thomas Ashworth, a local land surveyor, with works overseen by Jesse Hartley, who was the engineer who built Liverpool Docks. Wayoh Reservoir was built later in 1876, though much enlarged in 1962 when its capacity was doubled. They were built by Bolton Corporation and together they supply 50% of Bolton's drinking water!

Nearby Turton Tower was built as a defensive pele tower in the early fifteenth century and it retains its stone castellated tower. In the north-west corner of the tower, the shaft of a garderobe projects from the main structure. The tower had three low storeys as evidenced by the blocked window openings.

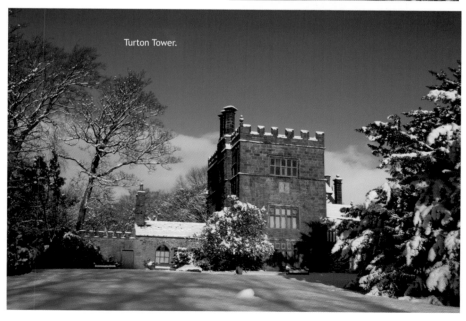

Turton Tower.

During the early sixteenth century two cruck-framed buildings were added to the tower and later an extension at the front of the house created the entrance with its imposing front door. Inside the building this Tudor architecture can be seen including part of the cruck structure along with exposed and restored sections of the wattle and daub and lath and plaster wall panelling. The entrance and entrance hall belong to the rebuilding of 1596 when vast changes were made and the tower raised to its present height. The new upper storey was built in stone. The old floors were removed and the walls raised to 45 feet to the top of the battlements. The narrow windows were replaced by large mullioned and transomed windows, transforming the appearance of the old part of the building. During the seventeenth century the cruck buildings were clad in stone and the structure remained unchanged until the nineteenth century. 1835 Victorian renovations included the Dutch gable façade.

There is a popular tea room here serving tea and cake. Turton Tower is now run by Blackburn with Darwen Borough Council and houses a museum. The railway from Blackburn to Bolton runs alongside and it is worth seeking out the castellated gritstone bridge over the railway which was built in a sympathetic style to complement Turton Tower. There is also a nineteenth-century water mill nearby.

There is a country park at Jumbles Reservoir. Jumbles is the most recent of all the reservoirs in this part of Lancashire, being completed in 1971. The circuit of the reservoir is a popular Sunday stroll and the café and information centre run by the West Pennine Moors Countryside Service offers refreshments as well as information on local history.

Jumbles Reservoir frozen over with a dusting of snow.

The Drop Inn, Top of Turton.

Bradshaw Brook is a lovely little hamlet of old weavers' cottages – such as those on Sink Row and Kettle Row – and is also home to a delightful little pack saddle bridge dating from the seventeenth century.

The locally famous Last Drop village is located nearby between Egerton and Bromley Cross. This was an old farmstead and outbuildings that in the 1960s were turned into a pub, restaurant and craft shops.

Nearby Hall i'th'Wood is an early sixteenth-century manor house on the edge of Bolton. It is a Grade I listed building and is currently used as a museum by Bolton Metropolitan Borough Council. It was the manor house for the Tonge with Haulgh township held by the Brownlow family in the sixteenth century. The original building is timber framed and has a stone-flagged roof; there were later additions to the house, built from stone, in 1591 and 1648. The name represents 'Hall

in the Wood' spoken in the local regional Bolton dialect.

Hall i'th'Wood was bought by William Lever (later Lord Leverhulme) in 1899 and was restored by Jonathan Simpson and Edward Ould. Lever gave the house to the Corporation of Bolton in 1900, yet another example of his philanthropic generosity to the citizens of Bolton and Horwich.

Hall i'th'Wood.

Looking to Hog Lowe Pike from the Beehive coke ovens at Broadhead.

Below: Looking to Peel Tower on Holcombe Moor from the Top of Turton.

A popular walk from Turton Tower is the climb onto Cheetham Close which offers grand views to Winter Hill and Jubilee Tower on Darwen Moor. Seek out the remains of a stone circle which suggests that early man also thought the view from here was worth celebrating. Unfortunately during the 1870s, a local farmer took a sledgehammer to what until that point was a well preserved stone circle. His motives were unclear. The stone circle is thought to be early Bronze Age and quern stones and arrowheads have been found during archaeological excavation.

These heights between Cheetham Close and Turton Heights were the gathering ground for the reservoirs owned by Bolton Corporation and their iron posts which mark their property boundary can be found strung out along the ridge top. Cheetham Close at 1079 feet offers good views across neighbouring Bolton and across to Winter Hill. It is named after Humphrey Chetham who was resident at Turton Tower for a time.

Short-eared owls hunt around these high tops in search of prey. This was once a landscape where golden eagles soared, the nearby valley of Yarnsdale means "the valley of the eagles". Such clues of wildlife lost can be found in other local place names such as Ousel Nest.

The valley through which the B6391 – Roman Road – runs was clearly thought to be of strategic importance as a lonely Second World War pillbox guards the entrance to Chapeltown, one of the few wartime pillboxes be to found in this part of Lancashire.

The scant remains of the stone circle on Cheetham Close.

Chapeltown is worth further exploration, particularly the High Street. A cross and stocks can be found in the garden of one house. Seek out the old school house, the Chetham Arms which dates from 1746, the old inn which is now a private house and a sixteenth century house. St Anne's church, built between 1840 and 1841, has an impressive spire which dominates the valley and is likely to be in view on many a walk around this area.

Excellent surviving examples of industry are the eighteenth-century Beehive coke ovens on The Naze. These stone built ovens are strung out in two groups with distant views to Hog Lowe Pike and are thought to be over 200 years old. The insides of the coke ovens are charred black from decades of use. Coal was mined throughout the West Pennine Moors and brought here to turn into coke. The coke in turn was used to smelt ironstone to create iron. Ironstone was quarried locally as evidenced by the name of Ironstone Delph on the edge of Holcombe Moor.

Below Turton Heights, the attractive little community at the intriguingly named Dimple is home to Walmsley Unitarian chapel which was built in 1712. The historic turnpike between Bolton and Blackburn was built in 1796 and passed close by.

Beehive coke ovens,
Naze End, Broadhead.
Inset: Walmsley Unitarian
chapel, Dimple.

Heron sculpture,
Turton & Entwistle Reservoir.

SUGGESTED SHORT WALKS

Entwistle and Yarnsdale (4¾ miles / 7.6 km)

Start from the United Utilities car park at Turton & Entwistle Reservoir. From the car park a short flight of steps heads down to the footpath that fringes the reservoir shore. Turn left on the good path that continues along the southern shore of Turton & Entwistle Reservoir. This winds in and out of a number of inlets, staying faithful to the reservoir edge as it runs on by a plantation as the reservoir narrows to the point where Cadshaw Brook flows in from Yarnsdale.

Spend some time exploring the permissive path that runs up both sides of Yarnsdale before returning to the footbridge over Cadshaw Brook. Climb up to a stile in the western corner of Fox Hill Plantation and continue over rough pasture on the Witton Weaver's Way. The Way doubles back sharp left and runs in a north-westerly direction towards Lowe Hill and a gate.

Joining a track head right to follow this good track as it winds through open country with long ranging views ahead to Peel Tower on Holcombe Moor.

The track drops down past farmsteads and by a charming whitewashed cottage to join a tarmac drive that runs right to Edge Fold and then continues as Edge Lane into Entwistle, passing eighteenth-century New Hall.

Edge Fold near Entwistle.

Edge Lane runs almost into the car park of the Strawbury Duck pub at Entwistle. Cross the railway and head left over a stile and downhill to cross Broadhead Brook at the northerly head of Wayoh Reservoir. The path continues in a southerly direction along the eastern shore of the reservoir to join a narrow lane.

Turn right on this narrow lane which runs on a causeway across Wayoh Reservoir.

The Cotton Mill Express crosses Wayoh railway viaduct.

As you reach Holly Bank at the western end of the causeway, turn left on the path beside the reservoir as it winds round to another causeway that offers superb views of the towering parallel railway viaduct.

On reaching the opposite bank, turn right to follow a permissive path beside the reservoir. This runs on beneath the tall arches of the railway viaduct to climb up through woodland and a narrow lane. Crossing this lane, a footpath leads into the car park where you started.

Turton & Entwistle Reservoir from Fox Hill Plantation.

Turton and Cheetham Close   (6 miles / 9.6 km)

Park at Turton Tower where there is a tea room and large car park. Turn right out of the car park to head past a watermill and a good view of the front of the pele tower of Turton Tower.

The rough track continues over the single line Bolton to Blackburn railway on a castellated overbridge designed to blend in with the neighbouring Turton Tower. Climbing away from the railway, the track splits and our way continues on the right hand fork through a gate to head along the bottom of a field parallel with the railway down below.

At a crossroads of footpaths, turn left on the Witton Weaver's Way to head across rough pasture below power lines, climbing across fields left of some farm outbuildings. Climbing a stile, the path continues up irregular steps into a thin stand of beech trees and out the other side.

With a gritstone drystone wall to your left and views across Bolton and Manchester, climb steadily alongside the wall to the wall corner and gate at the top. Crossing the fence with a stile, turn right to head in a north-westerly direction across the marshy, peaty top of Cheetham Close, heading directly for the

white painted Ordnance Survey column on the summit. A brief search amongst the rushes and reeds will locate the scant remains of a stone circle.

On the summit of Cheetham Close looking north to Turton Heights.
Inset: Turton Tower.

The Witton Weaver's Way continues across the top of the moor dropping down to an iron Bolton Corporation boundary marker. This spot marks the beginning of the descent as you follow a good footpath heading in a north easterly direction to a three way junction of paths at a wall corner. Take the path that slants down the side of the moor heading for the ruin, the lone sycamore tree and the rounded knolls of Three Lowes.

The path continues from here through a plantation to head north to a bend on the Greens Arms Road. Crossing over, a fenced path runs diagonally across the access road to Turton & Entwistle Reservoir, crossing over this access road to continue in the same diagonal direction into the car park. Turn right onto the road and then left onto the permissive path that runs alongside an arm of Wayoh Reservoir and beneath the tall arches of the railway viaduct above.

Bolton Corporation iron column on Cheetham Close.

Below: Curlew on Cheetham Close.

Stay alongside the shore of Wayoh Reservoir as the permissive path is joined by another path coming across the causeway. Continue alongside Wayoh Reservoir in a south-westerly direction towards the dam wall and the circular overflow structure, looking for all the world like a giant bath plug hole.

Wayoh Reservoir.

Turton Bottoms.

Turn left to cross the dam wall and at the far side turn right on the footpath as it climbs up to join the road in Turton next to the Black Bull public house. Turn right down the road and head downhill, before crossing the road to turn left into Birches Road, a lovely cobbled street with terraced houses running along its length.

As the road bends left, turn right on the footpath that runs behind houses to Pack Saddles Bridge crossing Bradshaw Brook. Turn into Vale Street to cross Bradshaw Brook again and turn immediately right on a footpath that runs behind houses to shadow Bradshaw Brook as it winds its way into Jumbles Reservoir.

Turn right to cross the concrete bridge over the northern arm of Jumbles Reservoir and climb steps to then gain further height, running on past a small pond. This is a lovely spot that offers views across Chapeltown with its iconic church spire. The path runs on to a Second World War pillbox guarding the B6391. Cross over and follow the pavement left as it runs on to the entrance to Turton Tower where you turn right to head back to the car park.

Pack Saddle Bridge on Bradshaw Brook, Turton Bottoms.

Looking to Holcombe Moor from Lowe Hill above Yarnsdale.

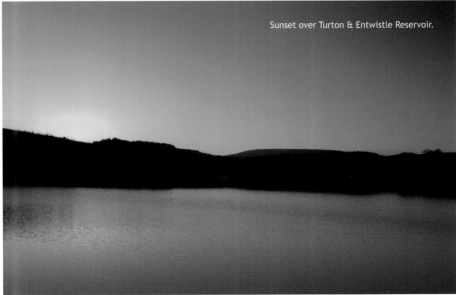

Sunset over Turton & Entwistle Reservoir.

Sunset over Winter Hill seen from Cheetham Close.

CHAPTER 5

BURY'S MOORS AND THE EAST LANCASHIRE RAILWAY

Duke of Gloucester departs Irwell Vale Station on the East Lancashire Railway against a backdrop of Bull Hill.

Below: Looking up at Peel Tower on Holcombe Moor from Chapel Lane in Holcombe village.

Harcles Hill and Bull Hill seen at dusk from Holcombe Moor.

Holcombe Moor and Harcles Hill draw ramblers and walkers from Bury and Ramsbottom. Peel Tower looms large over Ramsbottom and is yet another example of that north country habit of building great stone edifices on top of moorland heights. There are plenty of other examples across Lancashire and Yorkshire: Rivington Pike, Jubilee Tower, Peel Tower and Stoodley Pike being the most famous examples.

A part of this landscape is still used by the military around Holcombe Moor and Bull Hill. It can be closed when the firing range is in use so it is advisable to check ahead with the firing range and to look out for red flags flying which indicate that it is not safe to enter.

The Pilgrim's Cross close to Harcles Hill stands on the site of an ancient pilgrim's cross. There is a record of a cross here on this old pilgrim route as long ago as 1176. It was certainly mentioned in charters in both 1176 and 1225. The cross stands on an ancient route to Whalley Abbey near Clitheroe and it is thought that pilgrims would break their journey here for prayer. The cross itself is long gone and the socket stone remained on site until 1901, just before the current square cut stone was put in its place.

The Pilgrim's Cross on Holcombe Moor.

Holcombe Moor is now in the care of the National Trust. It was gifted by the Ministry of Defence in 1994. The nearby Stubbins Estate was acquired by the National Trust during the Second World War in 1943. It is incredible that during a time of conflict, the National Trust was expanding its portfolio, but it is perhaps an indicator of the retreat of the old establishment and the forward thinking that was already taking place for the end of the conflict that would ultimately lead to the formation of the National Parks.

At 1371 feet Bull Hill is a relatively modest height, but it is the second highest summit after Winter Hill in the West Pennine landscape and offers distant views to Pendle Hill and Ingleborough, as well as the Wharfedale mountains of Buckden Pike and Great Whernside, Snowdonia, the Peak District and the Lakeland Fells. There aren't many places in Britain where you can stand on a hill and take in distant views of four of our National Parks. Its higher neighbour Winter Hill dominates the view though.

Just below Bull Hill is a cairn and standing stone marked with the letters E S. This is the grave of Ellen Strange who was murdered on this hill long ago. Nearby is Robin Hood's Well, once of many places in Lancashire and Yorkshire associated with the legendary outlaw.

Bull Hill seen from Holcombe Moor at dusk.

Sunset over Winter Hill seen from Holcombe Moor.

A Jinty locomotive works away from Summerseat Station on the East Lancashire Railway with a train for Bury.

Below: Peel Tower on Holcombe Moor.

Peel Tower on Holcombe Moor seen from Summerseat in winter.

The small village of Holcombe is an attractive settlement nestling below the eastern slopes of Holcombe Moor and a useful launch pad for the climb up to Peel Tower. The village contains a number of old handloom weavers' cottages dating to the seventeenth and eighteenth centuries and the area around Moorbottom Road is particularly appealing.

Peel Tower on Holcombe Moor dominates the landscape in much the same way as Jubilee Tower on Darwen Moor does. It was built much earlier, however,

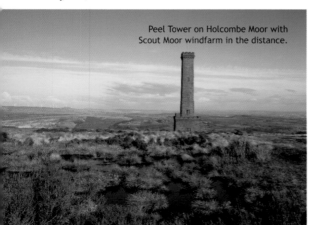

Peel Tower on Holcombe Moor with Scout Moor windfarm in the distance.

in 1851 and is a solid, strong gritstone edifice, 128 feet high and at an altitude of 1100 feet. It is named after Sir Robert Peel, born in 1788 in nearby Bury. He is most famous as the father of the modern police force. That is why police officers today are still known as 'bobbies'. Peel's greatest contribution to working class society though was his part in the Repeal of the Corn Laws, helping to reduce the price of bread, a basic staple of the working class diet.

A Santa Special on the East Lancashire Railway at Burrs Country Park.

The River Irwell runs north to south through this landscape. It rises at Irwell Springs on Deerplay Moor, approximately 1.5 miles (2.4 km) north of Bacup. The River Irwell runs for 39 miles through Lancashire before it empties into the River Mersey near Irlam.

The river became severely polluted by industrial waste in the Industrial Revolution, but in the second half of the twentieth century a number of initiatives were implemented to improve water quality, restock it with fish and create a diverse environment for wildlife. It is now home to kingfishers, salmon and potentially otters.

Running alongside and over the River Irwell is the East Lancashire Railway. This is a 12½ mile long heritage railway that runs from Heywood to Rawtenstall with intermediate stations at Bury Bolton Street, Burrs Country Park, Summerseat, Ramsbottom and Irwell Vale.

Passenger services between Bury and Rawtenstall were withdrawn by British Rail on 3 June 1972. Coal services to Rawtenstall ended in 1980, and formal closure followed in 1982. The East Lancashire Railway Trust reopened the line on 25 July 1987. The initial service operated between Bury and Ramsbottom, via Summerseat. In 1991 the service was extended northwards from Ramsbottom to reach Rawtenstall, via Irwell Vale. The railway is now a thriving steam-operated heritage line with weekend services throughout the year and weekday services in the high spring and summer season.

The stations on the northern sections of the line offer great places to start a hike up onto the West Pennine Moors and when you're up on the high moors, you can often hear the sound of steam trains down in the valley as they climb up the gradient towards Ramsbottom and Rawtenstall. On colder days, the columns of steam and exhaust help pinpoint the railway from the high ground.

SUGGESTED SHORT WALKS

Holcombe Moor and Peel Tower (5 miles / 8 km)

Note: This walk takes advantage of public access to Holcombe Moor military firing range. Check in advance that firing is not taking place and that the range is open to the public. If the red flags are flying, do not enter.

Holcombe Moor and Red Brook valley seen from the firing range.

This walk starts from Peel Tower / Holcombe Moor car park on the B6214 at Holcombe. Take the permissive path that climbs across a field to cobbled Holcombe Old Road and turn right to the junction with Moorbottom Road. Turn left on Moorbottom Road, but almost immediately take the path on the right-hand side that bends left and then slants up the side of Holcombe Moor past old quarry workings and through heather.

At the top, close to Top o'th'Moor Farm, a broad track runs back to the stone edifice of Peel Tower. Having explored the environs of the tower, a path leads on past the deep bowl beside the tower to cross the fence at a stile. Head in a northerly direction to drop down into a small defile before climbing up again to skirt the south-western flank of Harcles Hill.

At a fork, take the right-hand branch which runs along the western edge of Holcombe Moor above Red Brook valley. The path for now stays outside the military firing range, but our onward route strays into it, so make sure that the firing range is open to the public and that the red flags are not flying.

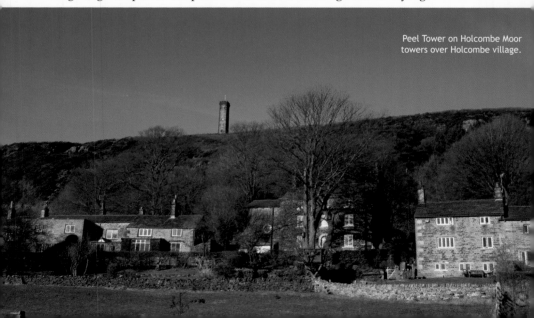

Peel Tower on Holcombe Moor towers over Holcombe village.

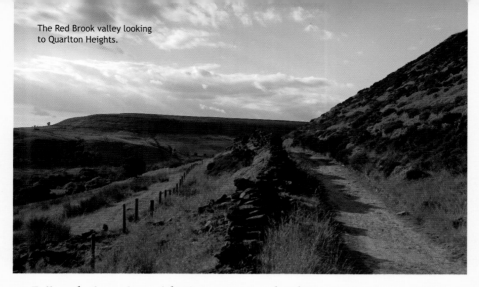
The Red Brook valley looking to Quarlton Heights.

Follow the boundary of the firing range with White Hill over to the right until you meet the site of the Pilgrim's Cross, now marked by a rather solid, squat stone slab. At the path crossroads by the Pilgrim's Cross take the path heading in a north westerly direction into the military firing range that climbs to the Ordnance Survey column on Bull Hill. This offers wide ranging views that include Ingleborough in the York-shire Dales and the high moorland tops of the West Pennine Moors. Winter Hill is dominant in the west.

An old vaccary wall, Red Brook valley below Holcombe Moor.

Retrace your steps to the Pilgrim's Cross and then head south alongside the moorland edge to begin a descent down into the Red Brook valley. The path drops down quickly to reach a track that has come around from the head of the valley. It's worth walking a few yards north to view the cascade on the right hand side coming down from the moorland heights.

Otherwise, turn left along this stony track as it contours along the side of Red Brook valley with Holcombe Moor above. The track passes various ruins and through various sets of gates until it passes Taylor's Farm. Stay with the track as it becomes Moorbottom Road, passing in turn the farmstead at Bank Top, then Hey House Mews, Meadow Heys and then Hill End Farm.

Moorbottom Road then meets Old Holcombe Road where you locate the permissive field path you used at the start of the walk to return to the car park.

A Black 5 locomotive passes Strongstry on the East Lancashire Railway with a train for Bury.

Irwell Vale and Alden Clough (5½ miles / 8.8 km)

This walk starts from Irwell Vale Railway Station on the East Lancashire Railway where there is a small parking area. Alternatively you could catch the steam train to start the walk.

From the station, turn left out of the entrance to then turn left by the small turning area to walk through Irwell Vale. The road runs parallel with the River Irwell alongside houses to the road bridge over the River Irwell.

Where the road bends right to cross the Irwell, don't cross the river, but continue straight ahead on a footpath that runs to a subway under the railway line. You have a choice of routes here. You can either climb up onto the trackbed of the old Stubbins Junction to Accrington railway line which is now a footpath and cycle route and follow this south for one kilometre, or you can cross under the railway line on the track that then runs parallel with the steam railway before heading south west alongside the River Irwell. The path stays with the river as it rounds a bend into Strongstry.

Passing houses and joining a rough road, you head back under the steam railway and the footpath/cycle route option rejoins the main route here. Follow the Rossendale Way as it climbs up to The Cliffe. The path continues on up through this National Trust beech woodland. While the Rossendale Way branches off to the left across the brook, a permissive path through this Open Access land continues its climb through the beech trees to the B6214.

Peak & Northern Footpaths Society signpost on Beetle Hill.

The permissive path continues on the other side of the road alongside this clough to meet with the bridleway heading north from Chatterton Close.

At a 'crossroads' of ways, rejoin the Rossendale Way as it shadows the brook onto the open moorland of Holcombe Moor before running across Beetle Hill. The path continues straight across a junction of paths to run above the intriguingly named Goose Pits. The Rossendale Way runs into the gathering grounds of Alden Ratchers where water running off Alden Breaks and the appropriately named Wet Moss collects to form Alden Brook.

The Rossendale Way dog-legs around this gathering ground, crossing Alden Brook and then running through rough pasture below Springs Bank. The path joins a farm track that passes farmsteads at Fall Bank Farm and Halliwell's and then contours around to head directly for the distinctive outline of Musbury Tor.

At a crossroads of paths, the way turns right past Great Houses to head down-hill on a lane past Tor Side Hall and Moorfields, around right, left and then right-hand bends by Ivy Lodge to run on down to Alden Road. Turn left on Alden Road and then take the first right that cuts a corner to run down to Holcombe Road at Iron Gate. Crossing Holcombe Road and heading briefly right, turn left to take the footpath that leads on by Raven Shore to join a rough track. This crosses the trackbed of the old Stubbins Junction to Accrington railway line before dropping down into Irwell Vale for the return to the station and car park.

Inset: Alden Brook, seen from Goose Pits.
Alden Ratchers from Bull Hill.

Steam locomotive Leander works through Burrs Country Park on
the East Lancashire Railway with a train for Ramsbottom.

Irwell Sculpture Trail and the East Lancashire Railway (7 ¾ miles / 12.6 km)

This walk starts from Burrs Country Park on the East Lancashire Railway and
follows both the River Irwell, the railway and part of the Irwell Valley Sculpture
Trail through this landscape.

   The Irwell Valley Sculpture Trail extends over 33 miles along the length of the
river through Salford, Bury and Rossendale. It is the largest sculpture route in the
UK connecting local heritage, the landscape and communities.   This walk
embraces some of the clusters of sculpture and art that can be encountered on the
route.

   There is a newly-opened railway station at Burrs Country Park which is a great
place to start the walk. Take some time to explore the country park which is based
on the site of an old mill complex. There were two mills here – Burr and Higher
Woodhill cotton mills. Some remnants of this industrial past have been preserved
and incorporated into the country park, including a mill chimney, a waterwheel
pit and the mill floor. The Brown Cow pub offers refreshments and there is a
tearoom in the line of old workshops that are preserved on site.

   Look out for three sculptures on the trail – 'Waterwheel', 'Stone Cycle' and
'Picnic Area'.

From the railway station, head past the Brown Cow and the mill chimney to locate the footpath that runs north alongside the River Irwell. For a section the footpath also runs parallel with an old mill race which fed the waterwheel at the cotton mill.

You will be in sight and sound of steam trains climbing towards Ramsbottom as you head north and already Peel Tower on Holcombe Moor will be in sight. Look out for kingfishers and dippers on this rejuvenated river.

The footpath stays with the eastern bank of the river through a couple of wide sweeping bends to return more closely to the railway line near Springside Farm. Leave the river here and cross under the railway line to pass Springside Farm. Continue past Bank Top Farm and turn left to head in a north-westerly direction towards Lower Summerseat, returning more closely to the railway line again. The path runs through thin woodland and drops down to a footpath crossing over the railway.

Cross the railway and drop down stone steps to the lane below and turn right to follow this north alongside the railway.

Peel Tower on Holcombe Moor
seen from Summerseat.

Pass under the railway and turn immediately left by Summerseat Station to follow a rough track that runs parallel with the railway on its eastern side. This runs into Summerseat, a lovely old mill village that was used as the setting for the 1980s' TV comedy series *Brass*. The village was also the site of high drama in December 2015 when the River Irwell became a raging torrent after prolonged rainfall and the Waterside Inn that stood beside the road bridge over the River Irwell was swept away.

Plantation View, Summerseat.

Fortunately the bridge survived, so cross the river with the railway line on Brooksbottom Viaduct crossing the Irwell to your left. Passing under the railway turn right on a cobbled path that rises above the preserved terraced houses that featured in the *Brass* TV series. That path climbs up beside the railway where it plunges into Brooksbottom Tunnel. The path ascends to the right above the tunnel and swings left with the railway underground below your feet.

Meeting a track, turn right, staying with the Sculpture Trail to run beside the River Irwell before crossing it on a flat bridge. This old carriage drive – Nuttall Hall Road – runs north to join Bury New Road. Turn left on Bury New Road to merge with Peel Brow and cross the railway. Ahead is Ramsbottom Station over the level crossing and to the right is another piece of sculpture – 'The River'. The small, vibrant town of Ramsbottom is ahead should you wish to seek out refreshment and dominating this whole scene is Holcombe Moor and Peel Tower.

Don't cross the level crossing, but return back along Peel Brow to cross the River Irwell and turn left into Kenyon Street. Follow this through industrial premises to rejoin the River Irwell. Follow the river bank to a footbridge on a side stream and then cut across a field to arrive on Bolton Road North on the edge of Stubbins.

Cross this road and go straight ahead on Chatterton Road. This terminates by the River Irwell and a footbridge. Don't cross the river, but turn right to stay with its eastern bank as it winds into Irwell Vale. You pass two more sculptures 'In The Picture' and 'Remnant Kings' before passing under a railway subway and emerging by a road bridge on the Irwell. Go straight ahead on the quiet lane through Irwell Vale. On reaching the turning area with the station and level crossing on the right, go straight ahead behind a stables. Cross under the railway and then stay faithful with the River Irwell eastern bank as it winds back under the railway and then under Ewood Bridge road bridge. It passes under the busy A56 and then through a steel stockholding yard. Turning left at Townsend Fold the path crosses the river and turns right for the final leg into Rawtenstall and the terminus of the East Lancashire Railway where you can catch a return train to the start. On the approach to Rawtenstall you will note a preserved mill chimney and three more pieces of sculpture – 'Gateway One', 'Gateway Two' and just beyond the railway station 'Bocholt Tree'. If you have time to spare in Rawtenstall you might want to seek out Britain's last original temperance bar and emporium – Fitzpatrick's on Bank Street. This is a real gem and an example of a fast-disappearing alternative to the public house.

Looking to Pendle Hill across the flat top of
Musbury Tor from the summit of Bull Hill.

Cotton grass on Harcles Hill looking to Greater Manchester.

Below: Sunset over Peel Tower and Holcombe Moor, seen from Ramsbottom.

CHAPTER 6

HASLINGDEN GRANE: A DESERTED VALLEY

Helmshore Textile Mill.

Below: Musbury Tor seen from Holden Wood.

Calf Hey Reservoir seen from the Rossendale Way.

Haslingden Grane is a beautiful landscape. It was once part of the extensive Forest of Rossendale, a royal hunting ground established soon after the Norman Conquest and it remained a hunting forest until 1507.

Today in many ways though, this is a deserted valley where the march of the water companies saw the eviction of farmers and crofters to create gathering grounds for the new reservoirs of Ogden Clough and Holden Wood. These ruined farmsteads now watch over this peaceful landscape. It is perhaps a mark of how secluded this valley could be that there are tales of illicit whisky making in these farmsteads before the authorities moved in.

As happened elsewhere in Lancashire, the Lake District and Peak District, the thirst for water in the developing industrial cities led to a significant acquisition of upland Northern Britain as the gathering ground for the reservoirs being built by the municipal corporations. There was once a village at Grane, a thriving community of nearly 1300 people who worked at two mills in the valley. When the land was bought, the village and surrounding farmsteads were cleared leading to an exodus of people from this landscape. The church of St Stephen's in Grane was dismantled and rebuilt higher up the valley side on the edge of Haslingden. Calf Hey Reservoir was the first to be built between 1854 and 1859 followed by Ogden Reservoir which was built much later between 1903 and 1912. Holden Wood Reservoir was completed in 1897.

Musbury Heights Quarry chimney and ruined workshops.

Below: Helmshore Textile Mill.

Musbury Heights Quarry chimney and ruined workshops.

There is early industry too in the quarries of Musbury Tor. Musbury Heights Quarry was the source of kerb and flagstones for many of the streets of Lancashire. It operated until the 1920s. Some ruins of some of the quarry buildings remain, including a forlorn looking chimney. The remains of a tramway can be traced which carried stone from the quarry on Musbury Heights down to a standard gauge mineral railway that connected with the East Lancashire Railway near Stubbins.

Helmshore Mill is now home to the Lancashire Textiles Museum. The museum comprises two mills which were built on the River Ogden. Higher Mill was built in 1796 for William Turner, and Whitaker's Mill was built in the 1820s by the Turner family. In their early life they alternated between working wool and cotton. By 1920 they were working as condenser mule mills; and this equipment has been preserved and until recent times was still used. The mills closed in 1967 and they were taken over by the Higher Mills Trust who maintained them as a

museum. The museum was open for visitors and undertook carding and mule spinning demonstrations. The mills were certainly the most original and best preserved examples of both cotton spinning and woollen fulling left in the country which were still operational.

Helmshore Textile Mill.

Unfortunately, following the withdrawal of its grant from Lancashire County Council, the museum closed to the public on 30 September 2016 for an undetermined period. The museum had struggled in recent times to secure the necessary funding to maintain a secure future and its long term prospects are not certain. This will be a shame as it tells the story of Lancashire's cotton industry which made the fortunes of many industrialists and raised the status of cities like Manchester and Liverpool. There is a working steam engine which dates to 1846.

The Rossendale Way passes through this landscape on its journey around the former Forest of Rossendale. There is a useful information centre at Clough Head run by the West Pennine Moors Countryside Service.

The high moors of Haslingden Moor and Oswaldtwistle Moor stretch away towards Accrington and Burnley. Perhaps the most iconic landmark is Musbury Tor, which with its gritstone edge can offer a profile similar to that of its much taller cousin Penyghent in the Yorkshire Dales.

Musbury Tor from Helmshore Textile Mill.

SUGGESTED SHORT WALKS

Haslingden Grane and Calf Hey Reservoir (6 miles / 8 km)

This walk starts from Clough Head visitor centre on the Haslingden to Blackburn Road. A permissive path strikes out from behind the visitor centre to run across a field directly for Nab Hill, climbing up onto the edge of Oswaldtwistle Moor. Joining the Rossendale Way, turn left to follow the path in a westerly direction as it stays loyal to the edge. After passing a plantation, turn left over a stile to drop quickly downhill and head directly for the road – the B6232. Cross the road and turn left and then at the first opportunity on the right, join a path that heads downhill before swinging right and heading west.

The Rossendale Way swings left again to run south for a few hundred yards before heading in a south easterly direction towards Haslingden Grane. The path passes the ruins of abandoned farmsteads, evidence of the clearances that took place when this valley was bought up by the water authorities. The reason for that clearance, Calf Hey and Ogden Reservoirs is obvious as you look east down the valley.

Crossing a beck coming in from the high ground off Boardman Close, you head through a small plantation to arrive at a T junction of paths. Turn right here, staying with the Rossendale Way to cross a small stream and then continue over Hog Lowe Clough. Leaving the trees behind, the good path contours along the side of the high ground that holds Musbury Heights with the waters of Calf Hey and Ogden Reservoirs below and to the left. At a fork just after a stream, take the left-hand footpath and part company with the Rossendale Way to head downhill towards the dam wall.

Nab Hill.

The Rossendale Way in Haslingden Grane below Musbury Heights.

Stay on the path as it hugs the lower slopes of Musbury Heights and turns in a south-easterly direction until a path escapes left to give you access to the drive coming in from Tenement's Farm. Turn right on this drive to run along the shore of Holden Wood Reservoir and turn left along its dam wall to head north to the B6235. Turn left along the B6232 past the cemetery and then crossing the road, follow the track that runs by Holden Hall. As you reach the end of the cemetery, a path runs half left to skirt the lower slopes and at a three-way junction, take the right-hand path that leads to Clod Farm.

Head in a northerly direction from Clod Farm to a crossroads of tracks with Windy Harbour Farm just along to the right. Turn left here – rejoining the Rossendale Way – to follow the path by Picker Hill to another junction of paths. Take the Rossendale Way as it runs between Haslingden Moor and the massive Jamestown Quarry. The route crosses Deep Clough and runs on to Nab Hill where the permissive path used at the start of the walk returns you to the visitor centre and car park.

Musbury Heights, Musbury Tor and Helmshore (6 miles / 8 km)

This walk starts from Irwell Vale Railway Station on the East Lancashire Railway. There is a small car park here.

Leave the railway station and head across the turning circle into Aitken Street, crossing the River Irwell and running briefly parallel with the River Ogden. Turn left into Bowker Street and swing right with this street as it becomes Milne Street and leaves the little hamlet of Irwell Vale behind.

A footpath climbs away from Irwell Vale to cross the trackbed of the Stubbins Junction to Accrington railway line. This railway opened in August 1848, but closed as a result of the Beeching cuts on 5 December 1966. The path continues as a track past Raven Shore to head on to the B6214 Helmshore Road at Iron Gate. Turn briefly right, cross the road and then turn left into a short lane that cuts through to Alden Road where you turn left.

At the first turning on the right head uphill on a lane that passes Ivy Lodge, Clough House, Moorfields and Tor Side Hall to rise to the group of houses at Great House. Tor Hill or Musbury Tor is above and to the right.

At a crossroads of paths head straight on along the Rossendale Way as it runs west between High Moss and Green Height. Musbury Tor doesn't present its best aspect from this side – this comes later in the walk.

The 'Duke of Gloucester' passes the flat-topped peak of Musbury Tor in the autumn with a train for Rawtenstall.

Stay on the Rossendale Way as it dog legs below Burnt Hill, crossing Long Grain Water as it cascades down from Long Grain and Musden Head Moor. The Rossendale Way now turns north to march along below Barnes Height and New Biggin Height, before swinging to the right to run on to Rushy Leach. Ahead are the abandoned quarries of Musbury Heights. The Rossendale Way runs through the heart of this abandoned quarry and the remains of buildings and its lone chimney can still be seen.

Remain on the Rossendale Way as it slants down from Musbury Heights in a north-westerly direction to a footbridge with Ogden Reservoir below. Turn right here to contour along the hillside and continue along the path as it winds towards the dam wall of Holden Wood Reservoir.

Holden Wood Reservoir from the Rossendale Way.

Follow the path across the dam wall and up to the junction of the B6235 and B6232 on the edge of Holden Wood, now a suburb of Haslingden. Turn right along the B6232 Grane Road and just after Holden Place turn right onto the trackbed of the former Accrington to Stubbins Junction railway line. This is now a cycle route and footpath.

Head south along the old railway line between old mills. The path deviates briefly away from the alignment of the old railway to cross the River Ogden before regaining the trackbed on an embankment and arches. This runs high above the Helmshore Textile Museum, crossing Yarm Avenue to terminate at Station Road. The station closed in 1966 and was briefly the home of a collection of preserved railway locomotives, the embryonic origins of the East Lancashire Railway before they relocated to Bury Bolton Street.

Looking across Holden Wood Reservoir to Scout Moor windfarm from Nab Hill.

Continue along Station Road, crossing Helmshore Road to follow the no through road that becomes a footpath running alongside the River Ogden. You can either return to Irwell Vale via Raven Shore and your outward route or stay with the River Ogden for a little while longer, crossing under the railway line and emerging onto a lane on the outskirts of Irwell Vale. Turn right to return to the heart of Irwell Vale and the railway station.

Calf Hey Reservoir seen from the Rossendale Way.

Calf Hey Reservoir.

Below: Ruined farmstead in Haslingden Grane looking down the valley towards Musbury Heights.

CHAPTER 7
PENDLE WITCH COUNTRY

Craggs Dole below the Deerstones on Badger Wells Hill.

Below: Sabden Brook at dusk, looking up to Spen Height.

Pendle Hill and Pendle would have been little known outside of Lancashire had it not been for the events that took place in the villages and farmsteads around its eastern flanks in 1612. Since then it has become synonymous with the Pendle Witches.

There are as many myths and legends attributed to the story of the Pendle Witches as there are facts. In essence it is a sad story of suspicion, superstition, paranoia, fear and intolerance. And yet it now confers on the landscape around here a sadness and fascination.

Prior to that time Pendle Hill was part of the larger Forest of Pendle, not a wooded area, but an eleventh-century hunting forest with its origins in the Norman Conquest when large tracts of land (a forest) were set aside for the hunting preserve of the barons and lords that had supported William the Conqueror in his invasion of England.

Pendle Hill has also served as a beacon, one of a chain of beacons along the length of the country, where fires would be lit to signal from one beacon station to the next, allowing the rapid communication of messages. Pendle Hill's lonely isolation made it an ideal beacon site. It is a huge whaleback of a hill and in the summer of 1887 a large fire was lit to commemorate Queen Victoria's Golden Jubilee.

Looking to Pendle Hill and Barley Bank from Spen Height.

St Mary's church, Newchurch-in-Pendle.

Newchurch-in-Pendle is a good place to search out the story of the Pendle Witches. St Mary's church tower dates back to 1544 so it would have been a relatively recent construction in 1612 at the time of the events in Pendle, looking out across a dramatic landscape as the drama of the Pendle Witches tale unfolded. The rest of the church was rebuilt some two hundred years later. It is perhaps fitting that the churchyard holds the grave of what is said to be Alice Nutter one of those accused of being a witch. An eye carved into a stone on the church tower looks out across the landscape. It is said to resemble the "all seeing eye of God"!

Pendle doesn't overdo its associations with the Pendle Witches story, though the little symbol of a witch on a broomstick adorns the footpath fingerposts in this district and points the route along the Pendle Way. The local buses also carry a livery with a glamorous image of a witch riding a broomstick. The one other concession to marketing what little hype there is around the story is the 'Witches Galore' shop in Newchurch-in-Pendle, an eclectic shop that is worth a visit if walking in the area.

The farmsteads around Newchurch are at the heart of the Pendle Witch story. On Good Friday, 10 April 1612, Malkin Tower was the venue for perhaps the best-known alleged witches' coven in English legal history. The house was home to Elizabeth Southerns, also known as Demdike, and her granddaughter Alizon Device, two of the alleged Pendle witches.

On 21 March 1612 Alizon had a chance encounter with John Law, a pedlar from Halifax, who refused to sell her some pins. Law collapsed shortly afterwards and his son accused Alizon of being responsible. Alizon and her grandmother were summoned to the home of local magistrate, Roger Nowell, on suspicion of causing harm by witchcraft. Both were arrested and detained in Lancaster Gaol, along with two other women. Friends of the Demdike family met at Malkin Tower on 10 April 1612, allegedly to plot the escape of the four gaoled women by blowing up Lancaster Castle. Nowell learned of the meeting and, after interrogating Alizon Device's "mentally sub-normal" brother, James, concluded that Malkin Tower had been the scene of a witches' coven, and that all who had attended, including Alice Nutter, were witches. Eight were subsequently accused of causing harm by witchcraft and committed for trial, seven at Lancaster Assizes and one at York. This was a period of religious intolerance and current thinking is that the witches were practising 'the old religion', namely Catholicism. This was against the law and so practising Catholics had to hold their meetings in secret.

The location of Malkin Tower is uncertain. It may have been demolished shortly after the 1612 trials, as it was common at the time to dismantle empty buildings and recycle the materials. The building may also have been destroyed to eradicate the "melancholy associations" of the place. The official account of the trials written by Thomas Potts, clerk to the court, in his *The Wonderfull Discoverie of Witches in the Countie of Lancaster* mentions *Malking Tower* many times, but only describes it as being in the Forest of Pendle, a former royal forest that covered a considerable area south and east of Pendle Hill, extending almost to the towns of Burnley, Colne and Padiham.

Pendle Witch Country below Spence Moor.

One contender is in the civil parish of Blacko, on the site of present-day Malkin Tower Farm; since the 1840s claims have been made that old masonry found in a field wall is from the remains of the building. In *The Lancashire Witch-Craze*, Jonathan Lumby conjectures that the building was situated on the moors surrounding Blacko Hill, near to an old road between Colne and Gisburn. Local folklore in the parish holds that the remains of Malkin Tower are buried in a field behind the nearby Cross Gaits Inn public house; the tower used to be featured on the inn's sign. The primary evidence supporting this location seems to be that a hollow in the hillside east of the farm is known as Mawkin Hole. It has been suggested that this is the same place mentioned in the sixteenth-century halmote court records for the manor of Colne as Mawkin Yarde, described as being "in the north of Colne", but anywhere inside the manor of Colne would have been outside the Forest of Pendle, and the first Ordnance Survey map of the area, created in the 1840s, identifies the farm as Blacko Tower. The site is also several miles from any of the traceable locations mentioned at the trial.

Stansfield Tower on Blacko Hill, seen from Twiston Moor.

In 1891 local grocer Jonathan Stansfield constructed a solitary tower on the nearby summit of Blacko Hill. Today this is also commonly known as Blacko Tower, and is often confused with Malkin Tower. Although he claimed at the time that he wished to see into neighbouring valleys, historian John Clayton suggests that, aware of the story, he may have wished to provide the area with his own version.

Sadden Fold in the snow.

Barley village.

Another possible location is somewhere near the village of Newchurch-in-Pendle. Douglas claims there is "persuasive" evidence that an area near Sadler's Farm was the site of Malkin Tower; there were numerous reports of alleged witchcraft in the area, and it was in the vicinity of other locations named during the trial such as Greenhead, Barley and Roughlee. Others involved in the trials were known to have lived in the area; alleged witches Jane and John Bulcock resided at Moss End Farm in Newchurch, and John Nutter, whose cows were claimed to have been bewitched, lived at the neighbouring Bull Hole Farm. Demdike's son Christopher Holgate also lived nearby. But neither the deeds of Sadler's Farm, which date back to the seventeenth century, nor contemporary maps of the region mention Malkin Tower or any fields in which it may have stood.

Archaeological excavations have been undertaken in several locations in the Pendle Forest area, including Newchurch, but nothing has been found. A potential candidate for the lost Malkin Tower was announced in December 2011, after water engineers unearthed a seventeenth-century cottage with a mummified cat sealed in the walls, close to Lower Black Moss Reservoir near Barley.

Barley is a pretty little village sitting directly below Pendle Hill's Big End. It is popular at weekends at it offers the best launch pad for an assault on Pendle Hill and from here one can take a number of routes onto the top of the hill – either long and gentle via Ogden Reservoirs or short and steep straight up onto Big End.

Roughlee Hall, reputed home of Alice Nutter.

Below: Sabden Beck below Sabden Fold.

There are wonderful tea rooms that offer home cooked traditional Lancashire fayre, proper meat pies in a delicious pastry crust for example.

Before it became popular with day-trippers to Pendle, Barley was a working village, home to the farmers that worked the land around here, but also a part of the Industrial Revolution, with small cotton factories and handloom weavers' cottages. A large cotton mill was washed away during flooding in 1880 and the site was subsequently taken over by a waterworks as a string of reservoirs were built in the folds and cloughs below Pendle. Near the car park are the remains of another cotton mill, closed in the 1960s and two attractive rows of weavers' cottages.

The corporations of Lancashire's cotton towns – particularly Nelson – recognised the potential of this landscape to be a gathering ground for the water that could supply the towns as they expanded during the Industrial Revolution. Upper Ogden Reservoir was completed in 1906 and although quite a small footprint in the landscape, it is impressively deep. Neighbouring Lower Ogden Reservoir was built in 1914 just before the outbreak of war. Nearby, Lower Black Moss Reservoir was built earlier still in 1903. Today owned and operated by United Utilities, formerly North West Water, it still provides drinking water for the townsfolk down in Nelson.

Lower Ogden Reservoir.

The landscape around here soon gives way to moorland of which Spence Moor is wild and windswept. There are clues in the landscape here too of the flora and fauna that could once be found here. Boar Clough is clearly no longer the preserve of wild boar – these disappeared from the English landscape in the thirteenth century – and today it is a popular route onto Pendle Hill. It is also known as Whinberry Clough. Whinberries are an alternative name for bilberries and these still grow here today, a useful source of Vitamin C during a summer hike when they are in berry.

The Big End of Pendle Hill offers superlative views across Lancashire, taking in nearby Boulsworth Hill and Weets Hill, as well as the more distant Yorkshire Three Peaks, the two Wharfedale giants of Buckden Pike and Great Whernside, the Bowland Fells and Lake District Fells, particularly Black Combe in the southwestern corner of the Lakes. Longridge Fell, Beacon Fell, Parlick and Fair Snape Fell are particularly well seen.

Pendle Hill is of modest height. At 1828 feet it doesn't qualify as a mountain, it doesn't even come close, but its relative isolation gives it a sense of being higher than it actually is.

Big End also looks directly down on Barley, nestling in the folds of the rippled landscape below.

Ordnance Survey column on Big End, Pendle Hill.
Inset: Winter snow on Spence Moor, seen from Sabden Fold.

Looking towards the Nick of Pendle under a blanket of snow from Deerstones.

A popular and easy route onto Pendle Hill where the car does most of the climbing is the hike across the moor from the Nick of Pendle on the road that links Sabden and Pendle Witch Country with Pendleton and Clitheroe Country. The route onto Pendle starts near one of Lancashire's two artificial ski slopes, though snow cover for real skiing on Pendle is less common than it once was.

The landscape between Nick of Pendle and Pendle Hill is classic moorland, peat on top of gritstone and three distinct cloughs – Mearley Clough, Ashendean Clough and Ogden Clough carry water quickly down off the hill to the waiting becks, rivers and reservoirs below. Early man made this place his home above the wooded landscape below and there is evidence of Bronze Age relics across this moorland, including the pile of stones or cairn on Apronfull Hill, an oblique reference to the pile of stones being an apronful that a giant would once have carried.

The gritstone is most evident where it outcrops at the Deerstones on Spence Moor. There are two distinctive marks in the gritstone here that look like two giant 2-foot long footprints. They are known as the Giant's Footprints and local folklore claims that the Devil or 'Owd Nick' gathered rocks from the Deerstones to throw across to Clitheroe Castle when he was passing by on his way from Hameldon Hill to Apronfull Hill. Why on earth he would want to do that would be a mystery, but you can't help but admire the imagination of the folk who come up with these stories! Deerstones was actually an old quarry where gritstone boulders were hewn from the bedrock.

This is border country, emphatically in Lancashire, but clearly the top of Pendle was once the boundary between neighbouring estates as evidenced by the abundance of boundary stones, most marked with the letters W (for Worston) and D (for Downham).

Stone-built shelter on Pendle Moor.

As well as a triangulation column installed by the Ordnance Survey, the summit plateau is also home to a giant stone shelter erected as recently as 1983, and this can offer a welcome respite when a strong wind is searing across the summit. Not far away is the Scout Cairn, an expertly-built drystone column, built in 1982 to mark the 75th anniversary of the Scout movement and the principal objective of the Mearley Clough fell race which tackles Pendle Hill in a steep ascent from Worston, a round trip that is typically achieved within thirty minutes! On Mearley Moor there is another large cairn erected by the Clayton-le-Moor Harriers to mark the destination of another popular fell race, as a memorial to two of their members.

Sabden, below the Nick of Pendle, also has strong associations with Pendle Witch Country. It is also famous for its legendary 'Treacle Mines'. In the 1930s, a considerable body of folklore began to develop suggesting the mining of treacle around Sabden. This was fuelled by local newspapers adding to the urban myth about these fictitious mines. Mounds of earth adjacent to the road that climbed up to the Nick of Pendle were supposedly the original entrances and signs of excavation from the Sabden Treacle Mines.

Looking towards Pendleton Moor from Nick of Pendle.

The myth grew and grew and became increasingly embroidered with tales of boggarts and hobgoblins eating the treacle and that the area was best avoided after dark. The boggarts worked the mines alongside parkin cake weavers and black pudding benders.

The myth probably has its origins in connections with wells or springs which could often contain natural minerals that would coat the sides of the well in a dark 'treacle' like substance.

Sabden developed during the seventeenth and eighteenth centuries into a largely industrial village with a strong reliance on textiles, the largest employer being Cobden's Calico Mill.

An excellent place to conclude a tour of Pendle Witch Country is the country-side around Barrowford and Roughlee.

The Pendle Heritage Centre, Barrowford.

Barrowford is home to the Pendle Heritage Centre. It is housed in the seventeenth-century Park Hill, an attractive old manor house, and is run by the Lancashire Heritage Trust. As well as rooms showing life in Pendle from an age gone by, there is a permanent exhibition on the Pendle Witches. The centre runs an excellent bookshop with a wide selection of books and leaflets. There is also a lovely tea room and garden on site.

Barrowford is also the starting point of the 45-mile Pendle Way which runs a ring around Pendle. The Way was opened in 1987 and today its little Lancashire Witch signs point the way clearly around this fascinating landscape.

Barrowford is also home to an old toll house dating from 1805 and on the old turnpike from Nelson to Long Preston.

Looking down on snow-covered Sabden from Calf Hill.

Looking towards Pendle Hill from Roughlee.

Roughlee Old Hall is almost certainly the home of Alice Nutter, a relatively wealthy lady who found herself caught up in the Witches Trial in 1612. Roughlee Old Hall is a particularly attractive house dating from 1536, so it would have been relatively new at the time of the Pendle Witches drama.

If you're walking on a Sunday in this part of the world, seek out the Clarion House tea room. This venerable institution celebrated its centenary in 2012. It has its origins in the socialist movement of the late nineteenth century and early twentieth century when as well as seeking improvements in working conditions, the working classes were also seeking self improvement and engaging in rambling clubs, cycling and amateur dramatic clubs. The *Clarion* was a working class newspaper, but the Clarion groups that embraced these outdoor activity groups also needed a place for refreshment and so the Clarion House was born. Since those early pioneering days it has continued to provide tea and sustenance to cyclists and walkers exploring Pendle's environs.

Roughlee Hall.

SUGGESTED SHORT WALKS

Pendle Hill from Barley   (4½ miles / 7.2 km)

Barley makes a good point from which to start a walk with a capacious car park and plenty of places to finish with food and a drink. This walk is probably one of the more popular circuits of Pendle Hill, though there will be many who opt for the more direct, though steeper ascent from Barley.

Cross the road to head past the village hall at Barley Green and join the road that runs through the valley to pass the northern shore of Lower Ogden Reservoir. Stay faithful with this road as it becomes a track and heads deeper into Ogden Clough. Ignore all side paths and stay with the main track as it winds on past plantations with Fell Wood to the south to continue past the dam wall of Upper Ogden Reservoir. The track follows the northern shore of the reservoir. You are on the Pendle Way here as it climbs up through the intriguingly named Cat Holes and Fox Holes.

With Ogden Clough to the left, follow the path as it swings right after fording a stream to begin a climb in a northerly direction beside Boar Clough. It's interesting to speculate on whether this was once the haunt of Wild Boar. It seems unlikely given the lack of tree cover and the height above sea level, but this landscape would have been very different before deforestation. The clough goes by the alternative name of Whinberry Clough and in summer bilberries will be fruiting alongside the path.

Boar Clough looking up to Barley Moor.

Ogden Clough winds its way down to the reservoirs.

Stay with the Pendle Way as you re-cross the stream and head right climbing to higher ground. Before long we reach the eastern edge of Pendle Hill, our way indicated by a series of cairns and almost all climbing is now complete.

Having gained all this height, the done thing is to amble along the edge in a northerly direction to the Ordnance Survey column on Big End which marks the top of Pendle Hill proper.

There is a choice of routes back down to Barley. You can either head north from the Ordnance Survey column to the ladder stile by the wall and then double back slanting steeply down the pitched path that loses height quickly as it descends towards Pendle House. Another option is to head south from the Ordnance Survey column to then swing left onto a track that runs in a north-easterly direction, slanting down the slope in the direction of Pendle House. They are largely of the same distance and both require the same amount of descent. The more southerly path is likely to be the quieter of the two.

From Pendle House, stay with the Pendle Way as it leads you across fields to Brown House where you join a track that heads for Ings End from where it is a short stride into the centre of Barley.

On Pendle Moor.

Collapsed drystone wall, Upper Ogden.

Pendle Witch Country from Barley (5 miles / 8 km)

Barley makes a good point from which to start a walk with a capacious car park and plenty of places to finish with food and a drink.

Cross the road to head past the village hall at Barley Green and join the road that runs through the valley to pass the northern shore of Lower Ogden Reservoir. Stay faithful with this road as it becomes a track and heads deeper into Ogden Clough.

As you reach the dam wall of Upper Ogden Reservoir, head left to begin the climb onto Driver Height. The path heads in a more or less direct line in a south-easterly direction across moist ground to meet Well Head Road.

Turn right here onto the path that heads across fields directly for Sabden Fold, bearing left to reach the road where you turn left. The road runs on to a T junction at Lower Sabden Fold and you turn right here briefly along Haddings Lane and escape at the second opportunity on the right to take the field path that heads across the field to Lower Houses. Turn left at Lower Houses to follow the access drive back out to Haddings Lane. Turn left onto Haddings Lane and where the lane bends sharp left, continue straight on past the buildings of Higher Town to merge with the Pendle Way.

Sunset over Sabden Fold.

Stay with the Pendle Way past Tynedale Farm house and after the buildings turn left, again with the Pendle Way to follow this path to Bull Hole (one time home of one of the Lancashire Witches). The Pendle Way will remain your course as you turn right just before Bull Hole to head for Moss End, passing the track that runs to Faughs and continuing in a straight line to Newchurch-in-Pendle where you turn left onto Spenbrook Road.

Turn left to walk through Newchurch-in-Pendle, passing the shop and the church to follow Cross Lane steeply out of the village. Take the path on the right

Looking up to Apronfull Hill from Pendleton Moor.

that runs into the plantation to head above Barley Bank, on through the trees until you emerge on Black Bank. The paths runs on across Thorny Bank outside Heys Lane Plantation to start its descent at the end of the nab. Joining a track here, turn left to follow this rough track through Heys Lane Plantation and into Boothman Wood.

The track leads unfailingly back to Bridge End on the edge of Barley where you turn right to return back to the car park.

Looking across to Bank Hill from the Nick of Pendle.

Roughlee and Pendle Water (5½ miles / 8.8 km)

Start from the Pendle Visitor Centre on Colne Road in Barrowford. Head through the public park on the path that runs alongside Pendle Water. Cross Pendle Water on a small footbridge opposite the White Bear pub and then cross Gisburn Road (A682) to head up Pasture Lane alongside the public house.

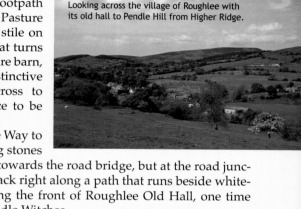

Looking across the village of Roughlee with its old hall to Pendle Hill from Higher Ridge.

Where Pasture Lane turns sharp left, continue in a straight line on the footpath that heads up the track towards Pasture House. Just after the allotments, a stile on the left gives access to a footpath that turns right and runs along past West Pasture barn, using the Pendle Way, to gain a distinctive brow with a superb prospect across to Pendle Hill. This is a superb place to be when the hawthorns are in blossom.

Continue downhill on the Pendle Way to cross Pendle Water on large stepping stones to reach Blacko Bar Road. Turn left towards the road bridge, but at the road junction just before the bridge, double back right along a path that runs beside white-painted cottages and then runs along the front of Roughlee Old Hall, one time home of Alice Nutter, one of the Pendle Witches.

At the junction of paths beyond, rejoin the Pendle Way by turning left towards Hollin Farm and on to the houses at Middlewood. Advance on the Pendle Way to begin the climb of the lower slopes of Brown Hill, but on reaching a junction, turn right to leave the Pendle Way behind and head along Hollin Top in a north-easterly direction to run alongside a plantation to Bank Ends. Continue downhill through another plantation, maintaining the same north-easterly line to reach Wheathead Lane at a bend in the road where it crosses the foot of Claude's Clough.

May blossom, Higher Ridge.

Rejoin the Pendle Way here having crossed the road to head along to the farm buildings at Admergill and beyond to walk alongside Admergill Water to the A682. Cross straight over the Gisburn Road and continue with the Pendle Way up a footpath that runs across Admergill Pasture. At the first opportunity, double back right on a footpath that heads due south parallel with the A682 and then bends left a little to run directly to Blacko Hill Side with the distinctive Stansfield Tower on Blacko Hill on your right.

Turn right at the buildings at Blacko Hill Side to follow the footpath that runs on to Brownley Park, but before you reach Brownley Park, turn left down a path that runs due south to Beverley. Turn right along Beverley Road to the junction with Gisburn Road and then turn left along the A682. At the first footpath on the right hand side, head in a south-westerly and then southerly direction to reach the confluence of Blacko Water and Pendle Water at Water Meetings.

Cross Pendle Water on a footbridge and rejoin the Pendle Way to run alongside the river all the way back into Higherford. Cross the road at Higherford Old Bridge to rejoin the opposite bank of the river and stay with this back to Barrowford Bridge, the Visitor Centre and car park.

Looking to Stansfield Tower on Blacko Hill from Water's Meeting.

Sabden and the Deerstones (5 miles / 8 km)

From the centre of Sabden follow Wesley Street and head for the tall spire of St Nicholas church in Heyhouses. Turn left to head on to Badger Wells Cottages and on to Cockshotts Farm. A path heads north with Churn Clough on the right. The path and Churn Clough part company as the footpath climbs further towards the left hand flank of Calf Hill.

At a crossroads of paths as you cross Badger Wells Water, head straight on, this time in a north-easterly direction to aim for the top left corner of a plantation. Stay outside the plantation as the path swings left to climb north towards Deerstones. The bowl of Craggs Dole is on your right.

On reaching the top of the edge, swing right across the top of this gritstone outcrop. Head directly east to climb a wall stile in the drystone wall and your path heads directly away across Spence Moor. The path heads in a broadly south-easterly direction, running parallel with a wall for a short distance before striking out again across the moor to a junction of walls between Cock Dole and Lower Dole. Maintain the same course until you meet the head of wooded Cock Clough.

Follow the path downhill, there is a choice, either outside the wall or inside the wall and within the clough. The paths lead down to the group of buildings at Sabden Fold where you take the lane south. Where the lane bends sharp right, continue ahead on a bridleway to the Old House and a footbridge over Sabden Beck.

Take a footpath on the right to the farm building at Drivers and another foot-bridge and ford on Sabden Beck. From here follow further field paths to Dean Farm where you pick up the bridleway that leads directly westwards to return you to the heart of Sabden.

117

Ling heather in bloom on Bank Hill, part of Spence Moor.

Below: Winter snow on Deerstones, Spence Moor.

CHAPTER 8

CLITHEROE, WHALLEY AND DOWNHAM

Clitheroe from the Castle Keep.

Below: Dusk falls above Downham village looking to Parlick and Fair Snape Fell in the Bowland Fells.

Clitheroe is a lovely little market town, bonded to Pendle Hill which watches over the town. In fact the view from the top of Clitheroe Castle affords one of the best views of Pendle Hill. The Norman keep looks out across the slate rooftops from the top of a limestone knoll.

Clitheroe Castle keep.

It's worth a stroll around the market town and visitors should certainly seek out Cowman's butchers, famous for the bewildering array of sausages on display.

Clitheroe Castle is a ruined early medieval castle, once part of a vast estate stretching along the western side of the Pennines. It is thought to be of Norman origin, probably built in the twelfth century. Today the buildings on the site are the home of Clitheroe Castle Museum. The keep is the second smallest surviving stone-built keep in England and is Grade I listed.

The valley of the River Ribble has formed a significant transport route for a long time; a Roman road runs up it, passing just south of the castle site. The steep limestone outcrop which rises 128 feet above the surrounding land is strategically located to effectively bar the pass and provide extensive views over the surrounding area.

It is thought that some form of fortification already existed here – possibly a wooden fortress – before the Norman Conquest, given the strategic importance of the site.

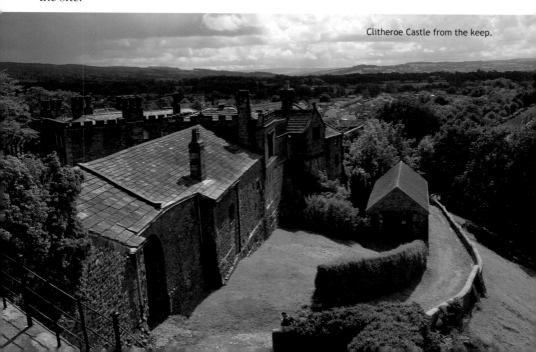
Clitheroe Castle from the keep.

During the early fourteenth century a new gate was built. In the fifteenth century, additional repairs were undertaken and a new chamber was built in 1425. During the Wars of the Roses, Edward IV ordered further repairs to the castle, but afterwards it seems to have fallen into disrepair. A survey in 1602 described the castle as very ruinous, warning that buildings were very likely to fall down, with another in 1608, stating that parts of the decayed buildings had actually collapsed.

Clitheroe Castle.

In 1644, during the Civil War, Prince Rupert left a garrison at the castle on his way to relieve the Parliamentarian siege of York. They repaired the main gateway and stocked the castle with provisions, only to abandon it following the royalist loss at the Battle of Marston Moor. When the Lancashire militia was ordered to disband in 1649, they refused, occupying the castle for a brief period in a dispute over unpaid wages. The same year Clitheroe was among a number of castles that Parliament decided should be 'slighted' to prevent further use, although it is uncertain what demolition work actually resulted.

Ownership of the castle subsequently passed down to the Dukes of Buccleuch. Around 1723 much of the remaining curtain wall was demolished with garden terraces created. The castle continued to operate as the administrative centre for Blackburnshire until 1822 when the town hall in Church Street was built.

In 1848, with the ruined keep in danger of collapse it was decided to undertake a series of repairs. The castle site was purchased by public subscription by the then borough council from Lord Montagu of Beaulieu in November 1920, to create a memorial to the 260 soldiers from the town who died in World War I.

The medieval castle keep and some of the curtain wall remain above ground, although the medieval buildings in the bailey have not survived.

The castle is known to have acted as a jail and occasionally important men were imprisoned there. Henry VI may have been held here briefly as he was captured outside Clitheroe in 1464, during the Wars of the Roses. In 1506 the porter was imprisoned in his own jail after attending a meeting of armed men at Whalley.

Pendle Hill from Waddington

Today the buildings on the castle site form Clitheroe Castle Museum. The museum is based in the former Steward's House, a Grade II listed building, originally built in the eighteenth century.

Pendle Hill in winter, seen from above Downham village.

The keep is on the summit of a large carboniferous rock, which is the highest and most prominent point for miles around. This is now identified as a Waulsortian mudmound. The rock comprises limestone with calcite veining. It is rich in fossils: mainly Crinoids together with gastropods and brachiopods. There has been much debate on how these mud mounds were formed; one theory led to them being called reef knolls, knoll reefs, or bioherms. Clitheroe Castle is the most south-westerly of a chain of mudmounds in an area dubbed the Clitheroe 'Reef' Belt. They include nearby Worsaw Hill.

The name *Clitheroe* is thought to come from the Anglo-Saxon for "Rocky Hill" and was also spelled *Clyderhow* and *Cletherwoode*. One claim to fame is that during the Second World War the jet engine was developed by the Rover Company here. Rover and Rolls-Royce engineers met at Clitheroe's Swan & Royal Hotel. The residential area 'Whittle Close' in the town is named after Frank Whittle, being built over the site of the former jet engine test beds.

Downham Hall.

Below: Pendle Hill from Downham village.

Limestone knolls abound around this side of Pendle Hill, the remains of an old tropical reef from 300 million years ago when this part of Lancashire was once at the bottom of an ocean teeming with crustaceans and small calcium rich invertebrates and coral. When they died, these settled on the seabed, the natural pressures compressing this silt into the limestone rock that forms the bedrock around here. It is still possible to find fossils – largely crinoids – in the stones that make up the drystone walls around the farms at the foot of Pendle.

Just north and east of Clitheroe is the street village of Gisburn with its bustling livestock market and a particularly nice restaurant. The remains of Gisburne Park – an old deer park once owned by Lord Ribblesdale – are close by across the railway with its castellated tunnel portal. Looking out on the road junction is the attractive church of St Mary the Virgin. It retains its Norman tower and incorporates some stonework from the dismantled remains of nearby Sawley Abbey.

Worsaw Hill from Worston Moor.
Inset: Crinoid fossils.

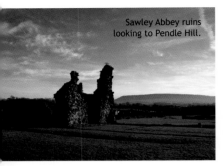

Sawley Abbey ruins looking to Pendle Hill.

Sawley or Salley Abbey dates from 1148 and was founded by William de Percy. It was a Cistercian Abbey, much smaller than the nearby Whalley Abbey. Today it is yet another of England's ruined Abbeys, dismantled during the Dissolution after King Henry VIII split England away from the Catholic Church. Sawley Abbey was one of the first to be dismantled as the Abbot had incurred the wrath of the crown for his part in the Pilgrimage of Grace – an attempt at a Catholic uprising. The Abbot was hanged for treason. Today Sawley Abbey is in the care of English Heritage. Like many others its stones found their way into local cottages and farms and in Worston village, one of the prettiest villages around Pendle, there is a house with three stone heraldic shields above the porch which are thought to have been plundered from Sawley Abbey. Nearby Little Mearley Hall which dates to the sixteenth century is also thought to have incorporated stonework from either Sawley or Whalley Abbeys. Nikolaus Pevsner described this attractive hall as "gorgeous", a fine accolade from the architectural historian who was notoriously critical of anything he didn't like.

Nearby Bracewell is a pretty little village with the solid looking St Michael's Church dominating this homely little place. It's worth a peep inside to seek out the carved mice on the pews, the handiwork of Robert Thompson, the famous 'Mouseman' of Kilburn in the foothills of the North York Moors. His craftsmanship has clearly spread far and wide into deepest Lancashire.

Pendle Hill from Pendleton village.

Whalley is the northern limit of our exploration. It sits just north of the River Calder and has two iconic landmarks – the impressive Whalley Viaduct (aka Whalley Arches), built in 1850 whose 50 arches carry the railway from Blackburn to Settle across the Calder valley; and the remains of the thirteenth-century Cistercian Abbey of which the impressive fourteenth-century gatehouse remains straddling what is now a back road. This rib-vaulted structure is now in the care of English Heritage.

St. Mary and All Angels Church, Whalley.

Whalley Abbey was founded by Cistercian Monks who had moved north from Cheshire in 1296. It was larger than its sister abbey at nearby Sawley. As well as the fourteenth-century gatehouse, another gatehouse from 1480 and the old dormitory are still intact, though most of the rest of the Abbey was destroyed as part of the Dissolution of the Monasteries.

The church of St Mary and All Angels is worth seeking out. It incorporates Norman features in the south doorway and inside can be found some fifteenth century wooden stalls that were recovered from the Abbey after Dissolution. An exploration of the churchyard will reveal three Saxon crosses dating from the ninth to eleventh centuries.

Whalley is a pleasing little village and a wider exploration on foot will reveal further gems such as the small group of old Jacobean cottages around the old Square.

A steam locomotive crosses Whalley Arches, seen from Whalley Gatehouse.

A steam locomotive crosses Whalley Arches with a special charter train; down below are the remains of the Abbey.

Right: Whalley Abbey Gatehouse.

Close by is the small village of Read. Read Park is an attractive former deer park, but perhaps of more interest is Read Hall, one time home of Squire Roger Nowell who was the notorious local magistrate responsible for rounding up the Pendle Witches for trial at Lancaster and York in 1612. The current building dates from the 1820s but occupies the site of the hall where Nowell lived.

Downham village with Pendle Hill shrouded in mist.

The seventeenth century was a tumultuous time for this part of Lancashire, for not long after the Pendle Witches trial the landscape around here was at the heart of some of the heaviest fighting between Parliamentarian and Royalist forces during the English Civil War. In 1643 a battle took place between Royalist and Roundhead soldiers on nearby Whalley Nab. Cromwell himself is said to have marched through this area and a small bridge over the River Hodder carries the name Cromwell's Bridge after the Commander of the Parliamentarian forces is said to have removed its parapets to be able to more easily march his troops, cannon and carts across on his way to the Battle of Preston in 1648.

Perhaps the highlight of the string of villages around Pendle is Downham. It retains an atmosphere from an earlier time and you will immediately notice the absence of modern paraphernalia such as double yellow lines or television aerials on the houses. This makes it a popular location for film and television as it takes little effort to transport the village back in time to another era. The popular

St Leonard's church, Downham.

Sunday night drama *Born and Bred* was filmed here and much earlier the 1961 film *Whistle Down The Wind* was filmed at a nearby farm at Worsaw End.

129

The road drops steeply from the top of the village leading the eye directly towards Pendle Hill. Downham Hall is a particularly attractive addition to the village environs. Dominating the top of the village is the church of St Leonard's, much rebuilt in Edwardian times. The Lords of the Manor were the Assheton family and their tombs can be found inside the church. Their name lives on in the Assheton Arms, a particularly lovely little pub directly opposite the church. The Assheton family bought the manor in 1558.

Downham village in springtime.

Spring is a good time to come to Downham when the daffodils will be in bloom on the verges that line the village street. There is an attractive sixteenth-century hall – Old Well Hall – with a two-storeyed gabled porch, so characteristic of the architecture of that time. This is now a particularly enviable place to live, though the cottages betray the fact that this too was once a busy little industrial hamlet as the windows indicate that these were handloom weavers' cottages.

The street leads down to the lovely little beck where on a warm weekend day, ducks will be dabbling, dogs will be splashing and children will be playing.

Worsaw Hill is a reef knoll, a limestone relic of a time when this landscape was formed from the silt at the bottom of a tropical sea. Subsequent glaciation has left a rounded hill of distinctive limestone character where crinoid fossils can be found in the drystone walls that ring its lower flank. This limestone landscape is a marked contrast to the peat and gritstone to be found on Pendle Hill.

Worsaw Hill.

Near the top of Pendle Hill is a small natural spring that looks out across the landscape of Downham and Worsaw Hill. It's a great viewpoint to absorb the attractive country-side around the River Ribble and perhaps it was this incredible view that inspired George Fox for it is here that in 1652 Fox had his great vision which was to inspire him to found the Society of Friends, also known as the Quakers. Today the spring is known as Fox's Well. In his journal he wrote "as I went

Looking to Yorkshire's Three Peaks from the Worston boundary stone on Pendle Hill.

down, on the hillside I found a spring of water and refreshed myself, for I had eaten little and drunk little for several days." Before that time it was known as Robin Hood's Well, which could be a link to the famous outlaw or more likely a link to the nature spirit known as Robin Goodfellow. In English legend, Robin Goodfellow, immortalised by Shakespeare as the character Puck, is often associated with springs and water. Pendle has clearly had a long association with myth and legend.

George Fox had been born in 1624, not long after the Pendle Witches' Trial and as a young man experienced the upheaval that came with the English Civil War through the 1640s. This was a time in English history when both the Establish-

ment – whether that be in politics or religion – was challenged by fresh and new ideas. At the age of nineteen, George Fox had already established him-self as a preacher, chal-lenging the established Church and its priests and offering a simpler take on Christianity and the teachings of Jesus.

Worsaw Hill and Yorkshire's Three Peaks seen from Burst Clough.

In the early 1650s he was travelling widely through Derbyshire and West York-shire and by 1652 he was on his way to Lancashire when, as he wrote in his journal, he "spied a great high hill called Pendle Hill … I was moved of the Lord to go atop of it." Fox recorded the ascent as "so steep" and "when I came atop of it I saw Lancashire sea; and there atop of the hill I was moved to sound the day of the Lord; and the Lord let me see atop of the hill in what places he had a great people to be gathered."

As Fox went on to found the Quaker movement, Pendle Hill became a special place for the Society of Friends and even today there is a Quaker study and retreat centre in Pennsylvania in the United States that is named after Pendle Hill.

Pendle Hill from Downham village.

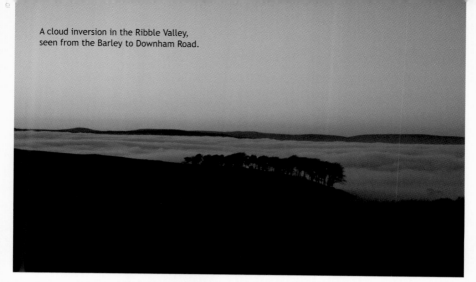
A cloud inversion in the Ribble Valley, seen from the Barley to Downham Road.

SUGGESTED SHORT WALKS

Downham and Rimington   (5 miles / 8 km)

The walk starts from the car park at the foot of Downham village. Walk up the steep main street past Downham Hall to the church and Assheton Arms and locate the footpath that runs on to the right behind the cottages. This climbs outside a small wood to reach the top of a ridge that extends west to Hall Royds Wood.

Head diagonally downhill across Downham Green to meet a footpath at the bottom coming in from the left. Turn right past Downham Mill to walk parallel with Ings Beck outside Falshaw Wood. Cross Ings Beck at a footbridge and take the left hand path at a junction that leads up to another path crossroads.

Turn right at this path junction to head along the top of a brow to a fork where you take the left hand path to head on to Stubs Wood. Turn left here to follow the footpath to Bustards Farm and then turn right onto the road into Rimington.

As you reach the eastern end of the village, turn right to take a footpath that runs across fields towards the farm-stead at Hollins. From here a path runs across the pockmarked landscape of the Skeleron Mines to reach a lane at Ings End.

Pendle Hill Big End in winter, seen from Rimington village.

133

Limestone outcrops, Downham Green.

Turn right on this lane to cross Ings Beck and stay with the road to continue straight on at a junction at Lower Gate and steeply downhill to Twiston Mill. Leave the road here at Twiston Mill by taking the footpath on the right that shadows Twiston Beck through woodland to a footbridge and crossroads of paths below Torrid Bank Wood.

Turn left over the footbridge to climb up the bank to the farmstead at Springs. Field paths run on from here via Wooly Hill to the farmhouse at Hey House Farm. Running parallel with Twiston Lane, a footpath continues over a crossroads of paths to run a permissive course behind Hall Royds Wood and along the ridge you first encountered at the beginning of the walk. This leads back to the pocket of woodland above Downham village where you turn left to return to the Assheton Arms and church. Return down the steep main street to the car park.

Old Well, Downham.

Pendle Hill from the Nick of Pendle   (6½ miles / 10.5 km)

Start from the parking areas in the old quarries at the Nick of Pendle on the road that links Pendleton with Sabden. The advantage of this walk is that the car will have done most of the climbing!

A clear track runs away from the car parking area towards Apronfull Hill and then Badger Wells Hill. The track forks with the right-hand path heading for Deerstones, while our route continues left towards Black Hill with Howcroft Brook in Ashendean Clough down and to the left.

The track runs on to join the left hand side of Ogden Clough. The path runs faithfully on with Ogden Clough for company and shortly after passing a boundary stone, cross the brook to climb on to Barley Moor and follow the distinct path as it heads directly for the Ordnance Survey column on the summit of Pendle Hill or Big End as it is also known.

From the Ordnance Survey column head directly north towards the drystone wall and climb the stile. Swing left away from the wall and stile on a permissive path that heads across the top of Pendle Hill offering grand views down towards Downham and Worston.

Looking towards Apronfull Hill from the Nick of Pendle.

The path follows the edge above Downham Moor and Worston Moor and continues to the large stone shelter and Scout Cairn above Pendle Moor. On meeting the wall beyond Turn Head, stay with the wall that runs in a south-westerly direction above Mearley Moor. Where the wall turns right, head down the slope into Ashendean Clough to meet Howcroft Brook and follow the waters downhill to another wall corner. Stay with Howcroft Brook to the footbridge above Howcroft Barn and then turn left on the footpath that climbs across Pendleton Moor to the top of the dry ski slope.

Turn left on the road to climb back up towards the car parks and quarries at the Nick of Pendle.

The Scout Cairn on Pendle Hill.

Worsaw End Farm, near Downham where *Whistle Down The Wind* was filmed.

Pendle Hill from Downham   (5½ miles / 8.8 km)

Start from the car park in Downham Village. Returning to the entrance, turn right to take the footpath that leads out across fields by Cat Gallows Wood and Longlands Wood. The path runs parallel with West Lane. As the path approaches Worsaw Hill ahead, it starts to head left towards Worsaw End where it runs ahead along the very bottom of Worsaw Hill. This is where the film 'Whistle Down The Wind' was filmed. It's also worth searching the drystone walls for evidence of crinoid fossils in the large limestone blocks that make up the walls.

Continue along the foot of Worsaw Hill to Worsaw End House and turn left to cross Worston Brook and follow a path across a field to a sharp right hand bend on West Lane. Walk straight ahead on West Lane and where it bends sharp right, continue ahead on a walled lane that becomes a rough track as it expires at the foot of Worston Moor.

A permissive path climbs steeply beside a deep clough and on reaching the top of the clough on Worston Moor, swings sharp right to run along to Burst Clough. This permissive path then climbs steeply up alongside Burst Clough, parallel with a wall.

Worston Moor on the flanks of Pendle Hill.

On reaching the top of the wall, the path crosses the head of the clough and runs diagonally in a southerly direction across towards the head of Mearley Clough on Pendle Moor. The path swings round to head in a north-easterly direction across to the Scout Cairn and stone shelter.

Downham Moor below Pendle Hill.

Stay with the edge path as it runs above Worston Moor and Downham Moor giving good views to the two villages below and across to the Bowland Fells to the north. The path stays with the edge before heading across the flat top of Pendle Hill towards the drystone wall and ladder stile close to the summit Ordnance Survey column. Climb the ladder stile to visit the Ordnance Survey column on Big End and then return to the ladder stile in the wall to follow the permissive path that zig zags down the northern face of Pendle.

This passes Robin Hood's Well where George Fox is reputed to have had his vision and swings left, then right, then left again as you rapidly lose height on the descent of Downham Moor. The path runs on beside a clough by Hookside Plantation and reaches Pendle Road at Lane Head.

Cross directly over the road to take the footpath that runs parallel with Pendle Road downhill beside a small beck. The path runs across the entrance to Clay House before continuing its journey to meet Downham Beck and then run on into Downham village.

Burst Clough on the flanks of Pendle Hill.

Looking towards Deerstones and Spence Moor from the Nick of Pendle.

Below: Looking towards the distant Bowland Fells from the Nick of Pendle.

BIBLIOGRAPHY

West Pennine Moors, Paul Hannon, Hillside (2005)

West Pennine Walks, Mike Cresswell, Sigma (1998)

Forest of Bowland, Andrew Bibby, Frances Lincoln (2005)

Walking on the West Pennine Moors, Terry Marsh, Cicerone (2009)

Walking in the Forest of Bowland and Pendle, Terry Marsh, Cicerone (2008)

Pendle and the Ribble, Paul Hannon, Hillside (2004)

www.westpenninemoors.co.uk

Rivington Terraced Gardens Trail, West Pennine Moors Countryside Service (1995)

INDEX

Sunset over the Pigeon Tower, Rivington.